SO-AWM-114

In the Feng Shui Zone clarifies the principle of energy through the ancient Chinese art and science of Feng Shui. Debra Ford has written this book in an easy-to-understand, logical style providing straightforward advice that is sure to change the course of your life.

Maureen Johnson, Student
Director, Johnson Group

This book is definitely a keeper! It proved to be the inspiration I needed in the darkest of times. I too have faith in the power of Feng Shui and what it can bring into our lives. With a little de-cluttering here, color there and placement of "stuff"— my sense of self is gradually returning. The transitional period I now face will be completed with grace, dignity, harmony and balance.

Roberta Smith, Student
Mount Royal College

In The Feng Shui Zone is inspiring. It shares a wealth of very well-organized knowledge. Thanks for the valuable information!

Angela Boze, Student
Mount Royal College

Debra Ford

In the
Feng
Shui
Zone

Good Health
Great Relationships
Abundant Prosperity

Copyright ©2004 Debra Ford

All rights reserved. No part of this publication may be reproduced without express written permission of the publisher and author, except in the case of brief quotations embodied in critical articles or reviews. Purchasers of this book have our permission to reproduce the Bagua map on the back cover.

Library and Archives Canada Cataloguing in Publication

Ford, Debra, 1957–
In the feng shui zone / Debra Ford.

ISBN 1-894694-26-0

1. Feng shui
I. Title

BF1779.F4F67 2004   133.3'337   C2004-905523-2

Editing by Diana Claire Douglas
Book design by Fiona Raven

Second Printing February 2005, Printed in Canada

Granville Island
Publishing

Granville Island Publishing
Suite 212–1656 Duranleau
Vancouver, BC, Canada V6H 3S4
Tel 604-688-0320 Toll-free 1-877-688-0320
www.granvilleislandpublishing.com

DISCLAIMER

The author of this book does not dispense medical advice or advocate the use of any technique as a form of treatment for physical or medical problems without the advice of a physician. The intent of the author is only to offer information of a general nature to help you in your quest for emotional and spiritual well-being. In the event you use any of the information in this book, the author and publisher assume no responsibility for your actions.

DEDICATION

I dedicate this book to the love of my life, my husband John — my biggest fan and greatest strength. You are the "wind beneath my wings." To my son Joel, who was bold and strong enough to step out into the Universe and believe that it would take care of him. To my youngest son Adam, you believed from the beginning. You are my hero. And to my mother Frances, who has the most beautiful personal energy. You have always been my role model.

ACKNOWLEDGEMENTS

I would like to thank all my students, who have in reality been my teachers, and my clients for trusting in the power of Feng Shui and for providing the examples in this book. I would also like to thank my dear friend Faye Gentry for believing. Without Jo Blackmore of Granville Island Publishing, my editor, Diana Claire Douglas, and my book designer, Fiona Raven, and their positive feedback and huge input, this book would have remained a dream. To all of you, my grateful thanks.

I am especially grateful and thankful for the power of Feng Shui to assist and improve all of our journeys through life, and I humbly share this knowledge with you. Pass this book on to your friends and family and assist them on their journey too.

TABLE OF CONTENTS

SECTION 3: GENERAL HOW TO'S

SECTION 4: NINE STEPS TO THE FENG SHUI ZONE

Preface

In the Feng Shui Zone will change your life. It's about using a "tried and tested" ancient Chinese art and science to effect improvements that you never dreamed possible. By using *In the Feng Shui Zone*, you will learn how to balance energy — the energy of your environment and your personal energy. You will learn about creating life success: abundant prosperity, great relationships and good health.

I have been asked many times how I came to be so involved with Feng Shui and I think that, in the end, Feng Shui reached out and found me. Feng Shui captivated me when I realized what it could do for my family and me. Like many families, we were struggling in jobs that we didn't like, with a pile of debt that was a battle to pay off, our sons were unhappy teenagers and we felt stuck. The more I studied, the more I could see the potential of Feng Shui to improve our lives and it quickly became my passion — my calling in life. There isn't enough space in this book for me to list the positive changes that Feng Shui has brought to our lives. Suffice it to say, on some days we have to pinch ourselves to make sure all the positive change is real.

I have had the privilege of studying under some excellent Feng Shui teachers in the United States and Canada. My most fulfilling hours have been spent researching and studying Feng Shui, searching for the answers to energy problems. In my studies I found that Feng Shui could be confusing, so *In the Feng Shui Zone* presents Feng Shui in a simple, easy-to-follow manner — an actual A to Z. You will end up with a clear Nine-Step Guide to getting your home and your life into the Feng Shui Zone. Feng Shui is many things to many people, and what I have hoped to do is demystify and simplify Feng Shui, to make it easy to implement so it can cause immediate change.

The examples in this book are all real-life situations that my students and clients have experienced. I teach Feng Shui in adult-education classes at a community college, write for women's publications, teach real-estate professionals how to work with clients who have Feng Shui needs (including preparing homes for a quick sale), provide office Feng Shui and decluttering services, plus do many home make-overs for clients. All of these experiences have provided me with the research data for this book. And they have shown me that there really is a solution for every Feng Shui energy challenge!

If you start at the beginning and work methodically through to the end of the book, your life will change in more ways than you can imagine. After you have read each section, make the recommended changes to your home. This is a book that should be read with a pencil and paper at hand, and a bunch of sticky notes too. Set up a Feng Shui journal to record the changes you are making to your home, and pay close attention to how these changes are affecting your life. I have mentioned many books and authors in the text who have inspired me; full references and annotations for all of them can be found in the bibliography. I have also personally developed a unique Bagua Map (adapted from the Lin Yun Institute), which is explained fully in the book, and is printed on the back cover. You have my permission to colour-copy the Bagua Map and use it in the many ways suggested.

In my experience, there seem to be three main reasons why people call me about Feng Shui: a lack of money, problems with relationships (spouse, child or other family member, co-workers, etc.) and health issues. And it is the same in all the countries in which I have consulted — Canada, the USA and the United Kingdom. Feng Shui can help with all of these life problems and many more. I have yet to work with a client and not see a rapid improvement in their life.

What we strive to achieve with Feng Shui is balanced energy. In a nutshell, this is how it works: If you balance the energy in your surroundings, this will balance and improve your personal energy; once your personal energy is balanced, the outcome of your life will be improved. In other words:

Balanced environment = Balanced personal energy = Improved life.

It's as simple as that!

There is an international spiritual reawakening underway, and Feng Shui is playing a part in it. *In the Feng Shui Zone* will help you improve your life and the lives of all who live with you. Imagine a neighbourhood where everyone has improved their lives — there will be more prosperity, happier families, better health. If we start with ourselves, move on to our families, our neighbours, co-workers, and they all do the same, we will all have an enormously positive impact on our world — one home at a time.

It is my privilege to take you on this journey to change the course of your life.

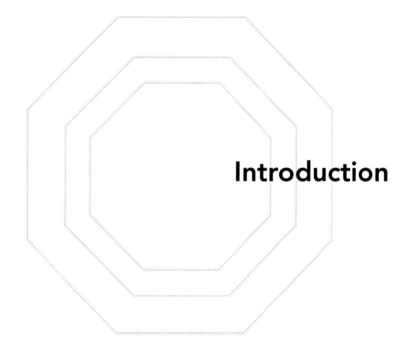

1

Introduction

1

Introduction

INTRODUCTION

In this section I will introduce you to Feng Shui by telling you what it is and what it isn't, by describing briefly its very long history and mentioning the schools of Feng Shui — especially BTB Feng Shui. I conclude the chapter by listing the benefits of using Feng Shui, sharing Mary's story and suggesting an exercise for you.

WHAT IS FENG SHUI?

Feng Shui (pronounced Feng Shway) is a technique for changing and improving your personal energy and the energy of your surroundings.

Feng Shui was the mother of the natural sciences in China, the original "environmental impact statement." By knowing the influence of . . . all the conditions of our total environment, we can help shape our destiny.

Steven Post, *The Modern Book of Feng Shui*, p. 7

Feng Shui, as literally translated from ancient Chinese, means "wind and water" and it is all about creating an environment where you live in harmony and balance with your surroundings. It is now understood in the West to mean:

- Feng Shui = Balanced Energy

- A description of how the energy of your surroundings and the energy within you interact to create positive or negative circumstances in your life.

- Tools and techniques for balancing, enhancing and changing the energy around you and therefore improving your personal energy.

What does Feng Shui do?

Using the principles, tools and techniques of Feng Shui allows you to create an environment where you live in harmony and balance with your surroundings, so that the energy around you works for you rather than against you. By balancing and harmonizing the flow of natural energies in your surroundings, you create beneficial effects in your life. Feng Shui improves the energy in your home and beneficially affects everyone's well-being.

What Feng Shui is not

A question I am asked frequently is whether Feng Shui is a religion. Not at all! I understand religion to be the formal institutional structure built around core sacred teachings. And I understand spirituality to be the personal experience of something greater than myself.

Feng Shui is not the result of any religious belief system, nor does it come into conflict with any religion. It is simply a way of knowing how your environment affects you and how you affect your environment. Thus, in order to practice and benefit from Feng Shui, it is not necessary to be religious or spiritual.

However, for some people, Feng Shui is a way to express their spirituality through their surroundings. Some trust that their strong spiritual beliefs enhance Feng Shui's ability to achieve harmony in their surroundings. Others believe, given Feng Shui's long and venerable history, that the thousands of years of ritual have accumulated power and energy. As users, they tap into this power and receive its benefits.

HISTORY OF FENG SHUI

The origins of Feng Shui date back to ancient Chinese nature-based practices. Three to four thousand years ago, philosophers in China started to realize that there was a connection between personal energy and the energy of one's surroundings. These philosophers dedicated themselves to the study of energy, as they felt that if they could understand the energy of their environment and how it affected them, they could change personal energy for the better. They felt that if everyone improved the balance of energy in their surroundings, they could improve their personal energy and therefore their life success.

In the late 20th century there was an invasion of Oriental practices into the West. First came Zen Buddhism, then karate and kung fu, then acupuncture, acupressure, yoga and Tai Chi. Finally came Feng Shui. The basic principles underlying these practices are the same — energy flows everywhere in the environment. And the environment includes human bodies as well as the entire Universe.

There are many schools of Feng Shui. These different schools came at different time periods, from different regions and different languages in China. Traditional schools of Feng Shui use a combination of Landform and Compass. Landform reads the lay of the land — contours, climate and shape — to find the best location for a building. Compass studies the direction of the front door — north, south, east, west — and compares this to your personal best direction, which is calculated based on your date and time of birth.

BTB FENG SHUI

Professor Lin Yun, of the Lin Yun Institute in California, is one of several teachers who adapted traditional Feng Shui for the West. He calls his style "Black Hat Sect" or "BTB" Feng Shui.

In his adaptation of Feng Shui, Professor Yun included influences from Western knowledge, natural science and architecture. He also merged Tibetan Buddhism and Indian Buddhism with traditional Chinese culture and philosophy, and included knowledge from Taoism, Confucianism, holistic healing, Yin Yang theory of balance and the I Ching. BTB Feng Shui combines contemporary and traditional knowledge to make modern living spaces harmonious.

BTB Feng Shui studies the individual characteristics of the site of the property. In our Western neighbourhoods, it is no longer important to have our homes part way up the mountain so that we can have a view of the valley to protect ourselves from hordes of marauding invaders. Nor is it of significant importance to most of us to be facing south (or north, west or east) so that crops will yield more. Instead, BTB Feng Shui takes into account the characteristics of the individual property, the location of the site within the neighbourhood, the position of the home on its lot and the factors within the close vicinity that are having an impact on the homeowners' energy or Chi. BTB Feng Shui also teaches the connection between the Chi (energy) of the surroundings and the Chi of the individual.

I have found BTB Feng Shui, adapted to our Western lifestyle, easy to understand, very practical and highly effective. I have also found that it is important to pick only one school of Feng Shui and follow its practices. Thus, the teachings in this book are based on BTB Feng Shui.

BTB Feng Shui teaches the connection between the Chi (energy) of the surroundings and the Chi of the individual. Each of us has a personal Chi with its own characteristics that maintains our physical and emotional balance. Using Feng Shui techniques will enhance the Chi in your surroundings to improve the flow of Chi through your body and therefore improve your life success. BTB Feng Shui combines modern and traditional knowledge to improve the places where we live and work.

BENEFITS OF FENG SHUI

Feng Shi is a simple, common-sense, practical approach that can be applied easily to your life — your inner life and your outer circumstances. There are many benefits to using Feng Shui. These include:

- Controlling the impact of the environment on your life.

- Transforming problems into successes.

- Manifesting new energy in your life.

- Enhancing your environment to benefit every part of your life including your career, wealth, health and relationships.

- Balancing and increasing the flow of energy in your life, thus improving your health, wealth and happiness.

- Responding positively to the flow of change in your life. Feng Shui can be used throughout your life, helping you to respond to the surprises that life brings you.

Mary's Story

When I first met Mary, she told me her life was a mess. Her relationship with her husband was in crisis, her communication with her children was non-existent, there were money worries, she hated her job, and she just couldn't get anything done. She just couldn't seem to raise herself out of her lethargy to make any improvements in her life.

A friend told Mary about my Feng Shui workshops. "What the heck," she told me, "I have nothing to lose. Feng Shui seems to be about energy and I definitely need some energy. My life seems to be going from bad to worse."

At the workshop and with a few private sessions, Mary learned what she needed to do to change her environment to increase the energy around her and to release her own energy. Six months later, she was feeling like a different person. Her relationships with her husband and children had improved wonderfully. The money pressures seemed to have eased — her spending was under control, there didn't seem to be as many unforeseen expenses as before, and her husband had recently been promoted. She felt better, had a lot more energy and was better able to cope. She was sleeping well (what a joy that was!) and consequently her health had improved and she felt happier than she had in years. Mary felt once again that she was in control of her life. She was in the Feng Shui Zone.

Mary experienced Feng Shui's simple, common-sense approach to improving all areas of her life. She learned that it was based on sound, fundamental, practical principles that are very easy to apply. By implementing the easy-to-follow steps in this book, you, too, can get your life into the Feng Shui Zone.

EXERCISE

I'll bet that you have applied Feng Shui techniques without even realizing it. For this exercise, remember the times you put furniture in a room and it just didn't feel right. You kept moving it around until it felt good — that's balance, that's being in the Feng Shui Zone. Instinctively you were applying the principles of Feng Shui!

Introducing the Basic Concepts and Defining Terms

2

2

Introducing the Basic Concepts and Defining Terms

There are several key concepts and frequently-used words that I need to define in this section so that you can follow what I am saying in the rest of the book. These include Yin/Yang, Chi, the Bagua, the Five Elements and Cures. There is an exercise for you to do that will start you on your journey to bring your life and home into the Feng Shui Zone.

YIN AND YANG

Everything in the Universe is composed of Yin and Yang energy — two opposite and complementary forces. These energies make up all matter. Yin energy represents the passive, dark side of nature and Yang energy represents the active, light side of nature. Nothing is fully Yin nor fully Yang, everything has the energy of both. Feng Shui is a way to balance Yin and Yang energy (using Feng Shui tools to be discussed soon). Balancing the Yin/Yang energy in your environment will balance your personal energy and will improve your life success.

WHAT IS CHI?

Chi (pronounced Chee) is an ancient Chinese word used to describe energy or life force. In many ancient traditions it was believed that there was a single unifying force or energy underlying all life. This energy was called — and is still called — *Chi* in China, *Qi* in Japan, *Prana* by Indian yogis, and *Life Force* by metaphysicians. In the West, modern researchers in energy healing are now calling this energy *subtle life-energy* or *bioelectromagnetic energy*.

For some of you, the idea that energy or Chi underlies all life may be new. In the West we have been schooled into believing that only something that is physically manifest is real. And since we can't see Chi or energy, we don't really understand what it is. Energy is the invisible but proven substance that is common to all living things. It is critical to life.

To be alive means to create, use and exchange energy. There are many forms of energy — human bodies use muscular energy to move, chemical energy to digest and electrical energy to think. In the environment, for example, energy takes the form of light, sound and heat. Chi unifies and underlies all these energies.

Traditional Western thinking has us believe that only living things — people, animals, plants — have energy. However, ancient wisdom has taught us, and modern science is "proving" that everything has energy, even inanimate objects such as chairs, tables and clothing. This energy changes depending on colour, shape and what the item is made of. For instance, you can feel how a round, wooden table has a significantly different energy than a square, metal table.

Throughout this book I will be referring to both personal Chi — the flow of energy within the individual — and environmental Chi — the flow of energy in our surroundings. I will also be talking about energy fields. This is the area of radiated energy given off by a person, plant, animal, etc. In the next section there is an exercise for you to measure another person's personal energy field.

What can happen with Chi

Chi should flow in the same way a babbling brook or gentle breeze would flow. When it is not flowing we feel blocked, unhealthy and unhappy. When it is flowing properly we feel happy, creative and successful. The physical environment — colours, shapes, lighting, etc. - affects the flow of Chi. This flow, or lack of flow, affects you all the time. By moving the energy and stimulating the flow of Chi you can improve all areas of your life. When the energy is stuck or stagnant your personal Chi will be stuck or stagnant too. Our task is to improve the environmental Chi, which will have a positive impact on your personal Chi, and get you into the Feng Shui Zone to improve your life success.

Chi and Feng Shui

Feng Shui is based on the understanding that all things have energy — not just living things — and that energy affects you for good or (unfortunately) for bad. Feng Shui is about balancing energy; it is about balance in all things, about making the right choices in your home and life. Just as everything you eat affects your body, so every-thing you place in your living space — furniture, lights and fabrics, to name a few — affects you too. The implications of this are enormous as this means that your surroundings not only affect your comfort, but your personal energy and therefore your life success too.

I will be referring to positive Chi — Chi that flows easily through your environment and creates positive personal Chi. I will also be refer-ring to negative Chi — Chi that is blocked in your environment and is having a negative impact on your personal Chi.

Feng Shui is all about balancing and harmonizing the flow of natural energies, or Chi, in your surroundings to create beneficial effects in every area of your life, such as your health, outlook, decision-making and prosperity. Feng Shui provides the knowledge and tools to improve the energy in your home and thus affect everyone's well-being.

Exercises to Become Aware of Chi

1. The coat hanger demonstration of Chi

- Find a clear place to try this exercise — outside or in a large room where your Chi is not interfered with by other energy.

- You will need an ordinary wire coat hanger and a partner.

- Stand about 20 feet from your partner. Ask your partner to just relax.

- Using one hand, hold the wire coat hanger vertically at chest height with the hook facing toward your partner. Hold the hanger very loosely by the long side of the triangle.

- Begin walking slowly towards your partner continuing to hold the coat hanger very loosely.

- Notice when the hanger begins to move left or right as you approach your partner. You are now meeting your partner's energy field.

- Repeat this exercise, asking your partner to remember a time she was happy. Repeat again, remembering when she was angry or sad. How does the energy field change?

- Repeat this exercise using your pet as your partner. How big or strong is your pet's energy field?

- Repeat this exercise with yourself and a mirror. Amazing but true, the coat hanger will move for you too!

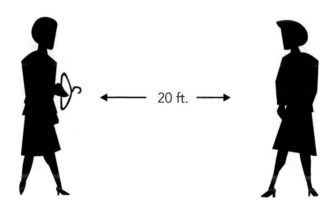

2. Seeing a tree's Chi

☯ Just before dark, go outside and find a big evergreen tree.

☯ Stand so that you can see the whole tree.

☯ Put your attention at 12 o'clock on the tree and then move your eyes to 1 o'clock. With your peripheral vision, look back to 12 o'clock. Voila, you will see the tree's energy!

WHAT IS THE BAGUA?

Developed in China, the Bagua is an eight-sided map of your environment showing how your surroundings affect different aspects of your life. The Bagua map is made up of nine guas (pronounced gwas), which I am calling zones. The nine zones on the Bagua map are:

☯ Prosperity

☯ Fame

☯ Relationships and Love

☯ Creativity and Children

☯ Helpful People and Travel

☯ Career and Life Path

☯ Skills and Knowledge

☯ Family

☯ Health

THE BAGUA MAP

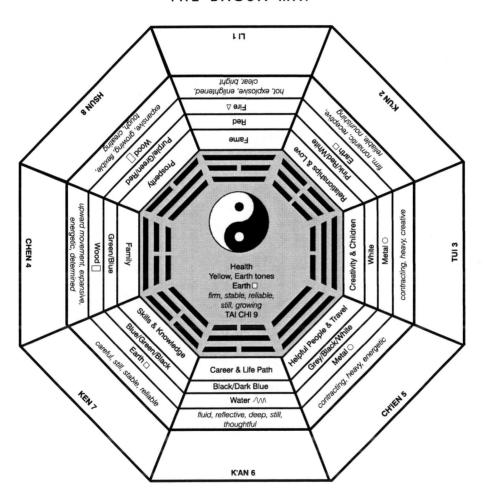

Reading this map of your environment, you will notice listed in each zone the following: the aspect of your life that it affects; the colours that will balance the energy in that zone; the natural element that needs to be placed in that zone; the shape, characteristics, number and Chinese name. Throughout this book I will be focusing mostly on colours and elements.

The Bagua Map and Feng Shui

The Bagua map can be used in your home, office, car, desk — any environment. The Bagua map is used to give you a guide to find the natural flow of energy throughout your environment and to balance this energy. Once you have the energy around you flowing freely, your personal energy will be affected in a positive way too. How wonderful! With only a few changes to these zones in your environment, you can make significant changes to different aspects of your life. Remember that the Chi (energy) of your surroundings affects your personal Chi and the Bagua is your map to make all this energy work for you.

FIVE ELEMENTS

The Five Element Theory was devised by the ancients to explain how the life force works. They believed that Chi in all its forms comes into and goes out of existence through the interplay of five natural elements — wood, fire, earth, metal and water. Feng Shui practitioners have applied this theory to balance environmental energy. This is done by using the Bagua map in combination with the Five Elements and making them work together. You will notice that each zone on the Bagua map has its own element.

On the following pages is a chart giving a brief summary of each element detailing its characteristics, colours and its shape.

The Five Elements and Feng Shui

As the chart shows, each element is a form of energy with unique characteristics, colour and shape. When the natural order of these Five Elements is used properly, harmony, prosperity and happiness will result.

WOOD

Element	**Wood Chi**
Zone	Family and Prosperity
Colour	Green
Shape	Rectangular (upright tree trunk)

Characteristics   Expansive, growing, flexible, tough, creating, upward movement, energetic, determined

Cures   Healthy thriving plants or silk plants. Wooden furniture. Wood paneling. Natural fibers e.g. cotton, silk. Floral prints on: upholstery, wallpaper, curtains. Artwork: landscapes, gardens, flowers. Green or 'tree trunk' shaped items

Building Element Water   **Reducing Element** Metal

FIRE

Element	**Fire Chi**
Zone	Fame
Colour	Red
Shape	Triangle

Characteristics   Hot, explosive, bright, clear, enlightened

Cures   Candles. Fireplaces. Bright lights and lamps. Things made from animals (fur, leather, wool). Pets. Artwork: animals, people, sunlight or fire (e.g., volcanoes). Red or triangular shaped items

Building Element Wood   **Reducing Element** Water

EARTH

Element	**Earth Chi**
Zone	Health, Relationships & Love, and Skills & Knowledge
Colour	Yellow
Shape	Horizontal, square, flat

Characteristics   Stable, reliable, firm, centered, receptive, nourishing, romantic, still, growing, careful

Cures   Ceramic or earthenware. Brick or tile. Artwork: landscapes. Earth tone items or flat, square shaped items

Building Element   Fire   **Reducing Element**   Wood

METAL

Element	**Metal Chi**
Zone	Creativity & Children, and Helpful People & Travel
Colour	White
Shape	Circular, oval

Characteristics   Contracting, creative, heavy, energetic

Cures   All types of metals including stainless steel, copper, brass, iron, silver and gold. Natural crystals, rocks, gemstones, stones (marble, granite, flagstone). White items or oval and circular shaped items

Building Element   Earth   **Reducing Element**   Fire

WATER

Element	**Water Chi**
Zone	Career and Life Path
Colour	Black, dark blue
Shape	Undulating, free-form, a shape that fills the space just like water does

Characteristics Deep, thoughtful, fluid, reflective, still

Cures Streams, pools, fountains and water features. Crystal, glass and mirrors. Items that are black (charcoal or dark blue too) and have a flowing, free-form shape

Building Element Metal   **Reducing Element** Earth

For example:

The energy of wood is growth. Therefore, add wood energy when you are starting something new (a new relationship, a new job), or when you are feeling tired or unmotivated.

The energy of fire is expansion. Therefore, add fire energy when you want to create more recognition in your life or improve your personal reputation.

The energy of earth is stability. Therefore, add earth energy to become more centred, feel more stable, especially at any time of intense life changes.

The energy of metal is contraction. Therefore, add metal energy when you want to improve creativity, communication and empower your children.

The energy of water is stillness. Therefore, add water energy when you want more peace of mind or you want to increase the flow of cash or people into your life.

BEING IN THE FENG SHUI ZONE

Feng Shui is all about balanced energy — actually Feng Shui is *only* about balanced energy. When you balance your environmental Chi (the energy in your surroundings), your personal Chi will improve and so will your life success.

Being in the Feng Shui Zone means that your life will flow more

5 ELEMENT SHAPES

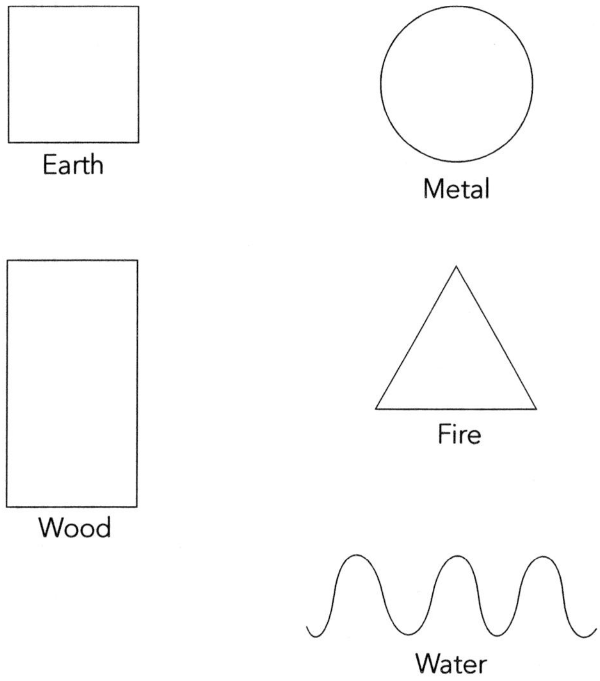

Earth

Metal

Wood

Fire

Water

smoothly (just as the Chi is flowing more smoothly) and you will have great life success. As changes occur around you — your economic factors alter, weather impacts you, other people make changes that affect you — you can make changes to your environmental Chi that will keep your personal Chi flowing in a positive way.

The reality of life is that it is a set of ever-changing occurrences. Being in the Feng Shui Zone — when your environmental Chi is balanced — will help you stay balanced and react positively to these changes. If your environmental Chi is balanced, your personal Chi will be balanced and your life will be successful, regardless of what is happening around you. The key to Feng Shui is keeping yourself in the Zone. As you reach a bump in the road, evaluate which part of your life is being impacted and adjust the energy in that part of your environment. I say more on this in Section Three.

Life is what happens to you while
you're busy making other plans.

John Lennon, *Beautiful Boy (Darling Boy)*,
Double Fantasy Album, 1980

CURES

In Feng Shui, the word "cures" is used to describe the remedies for imbalances in energies. Cures can be applied to solve energy problems, balance energy or enhance energy.

Cures are divided into nine categories:

- Light
- Sound
- Living Things

- Weight
- Colour
- Moving Objects

- Electrical Power
- Water
- Symbolic Objects

In Section Three, I will explain how and when to apply cures.

Cures and Feng Shui

You can enhance any area of your life by applying cures to that zone in your home using the Bagua map. Do you want to work on your health, wealth or happiness? Would you like to fix your money problems, find a partner or help your children through difficult times? Cures can be used to fix a problem, improve an area of your life, or strengthen an already-strong part of your life. Cures are used to balance the environmental Chi, which will improve your personal Chi and your life and the lives of all who live with you.

EXERCISE: GETTING YOUR HOME READY

To get you started on your journey of getting into the Feng Shui Zone, I have listed some of the things you can change immediately (before laying the Bagua map over your home), that will have an instant positive impact on your Chi. Even the smallest change that you make will have an amazingly positive impact on your energy — and on your life.

By doing the following tasks, you will also be preparing yourself and your home for more in-depth changes and balancing. Keep a record of the changes you are making to your environment and the changes that occur in your life as a result of using Feng Shui. It is easy to forget once the changes start happening.

Clear, Clean and Fix

Because we know that everything has energy, we are beginning to understand the effect that the negative energy of clutter can have on us. Below is a list of practical steps you can take to start freeing up the energy in your home by removing clutter. Don't think of it as cleaning and clearing, think of it as getting into the Feng Shui Zone.

- Clean out your clutter. Try to follow a 50% rule — all surfaces should have only 50% (or less) of space covered; all drawers must be filled only 50%. (This leaves room for good energy to enter your life.) A fundamental rule for clearing clutter — **If you don't love it or absolutely need it — throw it out.** Only have things you LOVE in your home. I had a client who was packing for a cross-country move and asked of every item in her home: "Do I really want to be moving you? Do I need you or love you?"

- Clean out all dirt and dust — everywhere. Cleaning will get the Chi moving. On a slow day in our business I have been known to get out the bucket and cloths; the energy picks up and so does business.

- Fix things. Make a list of jobs to be done, like replacing all the broken light bulbs. Start going through your list and getting things fixed.

- Throw out all dried flowers as they are withering and dead and are filled with dead Chi. This is one of the hardest things for women to do. I understand that they are pretty when you buy them, but now that you know they have dead Chi, perhaps it will be easier to throw them away.

- Ensure all trashcans have lids. Don't let your Chi, and consequently your money, go into the garbage.

- Clear out your garage, clean and lube the door and add light. The garage is a place that attracts clutter, so be especially diligent here. Don't let it become a rubbish dump.

- Clean all windows and have no obstructions in front of them and no clutter on the windowsills. Move furniture that obstructs windows. All the windows in your home should open easily and not be cracked or broken and there should be no bushes or branches obscuring them.

We've covered a lot in this chapter. You now know what the basic concepts and terms are in Feng Shui, how to start changing your environmental Chi, how this will affect your personal Chi and that your life will respond. We've started you on the course to getting your life into the Feng Shui Zone, by starting to clear your clutter. By now I'm sure that you will be noticing positive changes in your life too. Be sure to write down all the changes you are making to your environment and pay attention to the changes in your life. Changing and balancing the energy in your surroundings will improve your personal Chi and cause change for the better in all areas of your life — leading to greater life success.

3

General How To's

- How to lay the Bagua map over your floor plan
- How to read the Bagua map — the zones
- Understanding how the Five Elements interact with each other
- How the Bagua and Five Elements interact
- How to apply Cures
- Your Personal Chi Zones

3

General How To's

In this section I will explain in more depth how to understand the Bagua map, how to use the Bagua map in your own home, how the Five Elements interact with each other and the Bagua map, and how to apply cures. There is also an exercise for you to become aware of your personal Chi.

HOW TO LAY THE BAGUA MAP OVER YOUR FLOOR PLAN

The purpose of Feng Shui is to balance the energy in your surroundings, which will improve your personal Chi and have a positive impact on the success of your life. The Bagua is a map that shows you how to do this.

- Start by drawing the floor plan of your home. If your home is multi-levelled draw separate diagrams for each level.

- Divide your floor plan (on each level of your home) into nine equal "squares." Start by determining the front wall of the house — the wall containing your front door — and place the Career zone in the middle of the front wall (see diagrams at the end of this section). The Bagua map is set up in relation to the main front door (not the side door/garage door, etc. even if you currently use these doors more often). Your front door is called the "'Mouth of Chi" and it is where the main flow of Chi (energy) enters your home. On pages 42, 43 and 44 you will find diagrams of various front-door placements to help you lay the Bagua map over your floor plan.

- When you lay the Bagua map on your home floor plan, you don't necessarily need to divide rooms into different zones. What I mean is, if your living room falls into the Family zone with a smaller part in the Prosperity zone, decide that it is in the Family zone, where the majority of the room lies.

- It is also possible, if this works better for your home, to simply lay the Bagua map on each room (this is the best way to do a split-level home). Each room will then have a Prosperity zone in the back left, Health zone in the centre, etc.

- If you have a multi-level home, you need to lay the Bagua map on all the levels that you live in, e.g., main floor and second floor; main floor and finished basement. If you have a basement or an attic, which is mainly used for storage, all you really need to do is get it cleaned and organized. Use the Bagua map to get the energy moving on the floors that you live on as these are the floors on which the energy will affect your life.

- For the upper levels, or finished basement, the Bagua map is placed in the same direction as the main floor (the one with the front door).

FRONT DOOR IN CAREER AND LIFE PATH ZONE

PROSPERITY ZONE	FAME ZONE	RELATIONSHIPS AND LOVE ZONE
FAMILY ZONE	HEALTH ZONE	CREATIVITY AND CHILDREN ZONE
SKILLS AND KNOWLEDGE ZONE	CAREER AND LIFEPATH ZONE	HELPFUL PEOPLE AND TRAVEL ZONE

Front Door

FRONT DOOR IN HELPFUL PEOPLE
AND TRAVEL ZONE

PROSPERITY ZONE	FAME ZONE	RELATIONSHIPS AND LOVE ZONE
FAMILY ZONE	HEALTH ZONE	CREATIVITY AND CHILDREN ZONE
SKILLS AND KNOWLEDGE ZONE	CAREER AND LIFEPATH ZONE	HELPFUL PEOPLE AND TRAVEL ZONE

Front Door

FRONT DOOR IN SKILLS AND KNOWLEDGE ZONE

PROSPERITY ZONE	FAME ZONE	RELATIONSHIPS AND LOVE ZONE
FAMILY ZONE	HEALTH ZONE	CREATIVITY AND CHILDREN ZONE
SKILLS AND KNOWLEDGE ZONE	CAREER AND LIFEPATH ZONE	HELPFUL PEOPLE AND TRAVEL ZONE

Front Door

THE BAGUA MAP — THE ZONES

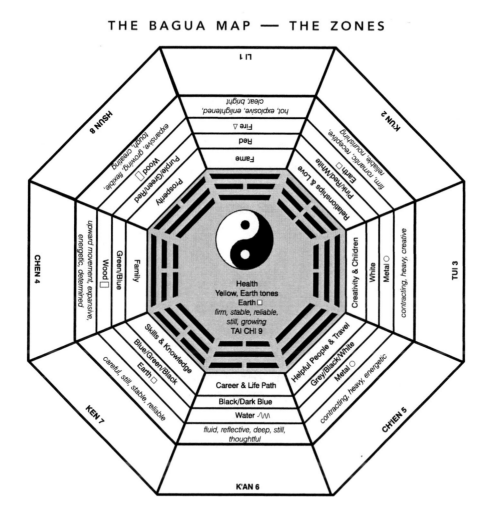

LI 1

hot, explosive, enlightened, clear, bright

Fire △

Red

Fame

HSUN 8

expansive, growing, flexible, tough, creating

Wood □

Purple/Green/Red

Prosperity

KUN 2

firm, romantic, receptive, reliable, nourishing

Earth □

Pink/Red/White

Relationships & Love

CHEN 4

upward movement, expansive, energetic, determined

Wood □

Green/Blue

Family

TUI 3

contracting, heavy, creative

Metal ○

White

Creativity & Children

Health
Yellow, Earth tones
Earth □
firm, stable, reliable,
still, growing
TAI CHI 9

KEN 7

careful, still, stable, reliable

Earth □

Blue/Green/Black

Skills & Knowledge

CH'IEN 5

contracting, heavy, energetic

Metal ○

Grey/Black/White

Helpful People & Travel

Career & Life Path

Black/Dark Blue

Water ⌁

fluid, reflective, deep, still, thoughtful

K'AN 6

Refer to the diagram on page 45 while reading the zone descriptions below in order to become familiar with the zone placements.

Prosperity

This zone of the Bagua map is located in the back upper left of your home. The Chinese name is Hsun. The prosperity area directly affects your financial situation and the abundance in your life (not only your cash abundance, but also your abundance of happiness, health, friendship, etc.). You can boost the energy in this zone by introducing the colours purple, green and red and the element wood. Other areas of your home that affect your money Chi are the front entrance and kitchen stove.

Fame

This zone of the Bagua map is located in the back centre of your home. The Chinese name is Li. Introducing the colour red and the element fire will boost the energy here. The fame zone directly affects your personal reputation and how other people see you. A good reputation brings many benefits into your life. Enhance this area if you are setting goals and planning your future.

Relationships and Love

This zone of the Bagua map is located in the back upper right of your home. The Chinese name is K'un. You will boost the energy of this zone by introducing the colours pink, red and white and the element earth. The relationship zone directly affects your relationship with your significant other and most importantly yourself. Enhancing this area will also attract new relationships.

Creativity and Children

This zone of the Bagua map is located in the centre right of your home. The Chinese name is Tui. Using the colour white and the element metal will boost the energy of this zone. This zone is directly connected to the health and well being of your children. Your creative energies are located in this area, as well as the quality of your communications — writing, speaking and listening.

Helpful People and Travel

This zone of the Bagua map is located in the front right of your home. The Chinese name is Ch'ien. You can boost the energy of this zone by adding the colours grey, black and white and the element metal. Enhancing this zone will benefit all your relationships and attract helpful people into your life. This area also affects your travel plans, increasing the likelihood of travel and making your travels safer and easier. Enhancing this area will make the biggest and quickest change in your life.

Career and Life Path

This zone of the Bagua map is located in the front centre of your home. The Chinese name is K'an. Using the colours black and dark blue and the element water will boost the energy here. This zone concerns your work and career success. Add enhancements to this zone if you want to find out what you want to do with your life, find a better job, be promoted or receive increased recognition at work.

Skills and Knowledge

This zone of the Bagua map is located in the front left of your home. The Chinese name is Ken. You can boost the energy of this zone by adding the colours blue, green and black and the element earth. The knowledge zone is associated with your spiritual life, personal growth, studies and self-development.

Family

This zone of the Bagua map is located in the centre left of your home. The Chinese name is Chen. The colours green and blue and the element wood will boost the energy of this zone. This zone concerns your immediate family, relatives, extended family of close friends and colleagues. If you need to improve relationships or resolve conflicts with people close to you, you need to enhance this zone.

Health

This zone of the Bagua map is located in the centre of your home. The Chinese name is Tai Chi. You can boost the energy of this zone by adding yellow and earth-tone colours and the element earth. This zone is primarily concerned with your physical and mental health. You will improve vitality, stamina and increase a sense of balance in your life when you enhance this zone.

UNDERSTANDING HOW THE FIVE ELEMENTS INTERACT WITH EACH OTHER

The Five Elements play a large role in balancing the energy in your environment — in getting your home into the Feng Shui Zone. Once again, these elements are Wood, Fire, Earth, Metal and Water. The interaction of the Five Elements is understood to happen in two cycles — the cycle of generation, which I refer to as the building cycle, and the cycle of destruction, which I refer to as the reducing cycle. How the Five Elements cause change, shapes your life. The Five Elements react with each other and represent how things increase or decrease, are created or reduced. When these Five Elements are balanced in your environment, harmony and prosperity will result.

In the building cycle, the elements interact with each other in this way: Wood feeds Fire; Fire breaks down into ash and feeds Earth; Earth creates Metal; Metal melts down to form Water; Water feeds Wood.

BUILDING CYCLE:

```
              ↗ FIRE ↘
      WOOD              EARTH
         ↑                ↓
      WATER  ←——  METAL
```

In a practical situation if you need to add the element of Fire, but the situation didn't lend itself to candles, lights, etc., add wood energy — because Wood feeds Fire. (For easy reference refer to the Five Element Chart (on pages 53, 54 and 55 or in Section Six: Resources.)

In the reducing cycle, Water puts out Fire; Fire melts Metal; Metal chops Wood; Wood penetrates Earth; Earth dams Water.

REDUCING CYCLE: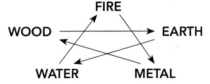

In a practical situation, if you have too much Metal (white) in a zone of your home, you can add Fire (red, triangular shapes) — because Fire melts Metal. Or in a room with wood panelling and hardwood flooring (too much of the wood element), you can add metal (any metal or white objects) because metal chops wood (metal reduces wood).

HOW THE BAGUA MAP AND FIVE ELEMENTS INTERACT

Feng Shui is all about balancing energy to get positive results and it is therefore logical that too much of one element causes an imbalance of energy and affects the Chi negatively. For example, a home that has too much metal feels cold and lonely, while a home with too much wood may feel dark and depressing. Your home needs equal parts of all elements to be in balance and have the energy flowing and get you into the Feng Shui Zone.

These elements help balance the energy in your home when you place them in their correct zones and as they interact with each other in either a building or reducing manner. The Bagua map is your guide to the placement of the Five Elements.

For easy reference, here is the Five Element Chart again. This chart is also found in Section Six: Resources.

WOOD

Element	**Wood Chi**
Zone	Family and Prosperity
Colour	Green
Shape	Rectangular (upright tree trunk)

Characteristics   Expansive, growing, flexible, tough, creating, upward movement, energetic, determined

Cures   Healthy thriving plants or silk plants. Wooden furniture. Wood paneling. Natural fibers e.g. cotton, silk. Floral prints on: upholstery, wallpaper, curtains. Artwork: landscapes, gardens, flowers. Green or 'tree trunk' shaped items

Building Element Water   **Reducing Element** Metal

FIRE

Element	**Fire Chi**
Zone	Fame
Colour	Red
Shape	Triangle

Characteristics   Hot, explosive, bright, clear, enlightened

Cures   Candles. Fireplaces. Bright lights and lamps. Things made from animals (fur, leather, wool). Pets. Artwork: animals, people, sunlight or fire (e.g., volcanoes). Red or triangular shaped items

Building Element Wood   **Reducing Element** Water

EARTH

Element	**Earth Chi**
Zone	Health, Relationships & Love, and Skills & Knowledge
Colour	Yellow
Shape	Horizontal, square, flat

Characteristics   Stable, reliable, firm, centered, receptive, nourishing, romantic, still, growing, careful

Cures   Ceramic or earthenware. Brick or tile. Artwork: landscapes. Earth tone items or flat, square shaped items

Building Element Fire   **Reducing Element** Wood

METAL

Element	**Metal Chi**
Zone	Creativity & Children, and Helpful People & Travel
Colour	White
Shape	Circular, oval

Characteristics   Contracting, creative, heavy, energetic

Cures   All types of metals including stainless steel, copper, brass, iron, silver and gold. Natural crystals, rocks, gemstones, stones (marble, granite, flagstone). White items or oval and circular shaped items

Building Element Earth   **Reducing Element** Fire

Element	**Water Chi**	
Zone	Career and Life Path	
Colour	Black, dark blue	
Shape	Undulating, free-form, a shape that fills the space just like water does	

Characteristics   Deep, thoughtful, fluid, reflective, still

Cures   Streams, pools, fountains and water features. Crystal, glass and mirrors. Items that are black (charcoal or dark blue too) and have a flowing, free-form shape

Building Element   Metal   **Reducing Element**   Earth

HOW TO APPLY CURES

Cures are remedies for your energy problems. They are used to solve energy problems, and balance or enhance energy in your environment. In BTB Feng Shui, the physical cure is said to influence the Chi by about 30 per cent, the other 70 per cent is influenced by your "intention" when doing the cure. (More about this in Section Four: Nine Steps to the Feng Shui Zone.)

Cures are divided into nine categories:

1. **Light. Electric lights, crystals and mirrors are light cures.**

- Lights add brightness and happiness. When placing a light cure, the brighter the better. Keep your home well lit so that it is welcoming and stimulates Chi. Adding light to your home increases Chi and brings positive changes into your life.

- Crystals add light and new energy and can redirect energy in a more beneficial direction. They can also protect you from chaotic and negative energy. Crystals come from the earth and possess healing qualities. They help harness the positive energy of nature.

- Mirrors add light and brightness and can attract new energy into a space. They can expand a space and magnify an image. They can be used to cancel out bad influences and get rid of bad Chi.

2. **Sound. Chimes and bells are sound cures.**

- Wind chimes can be used both indoors and outside. Chimes

attract new energy, stimulate opportunities and remove obstacles in your life.

◑ A brass bell can be used where a wind chime is not suitable.

3. Living things. Animals, fish and plants are living cures.

◑ Beloved and well looked after pets add vitality and boost the Chi of your home.

◑ Aquariums are powerful cures. They add vitality and stimulate energy flow. They create a sense of peacefulness and encourage wealth. Healthy fish and clean water in an aquarium will attract good fortune and wealth. Three, six or nine fish are ideal in an aquarium.

◑ Plants add colour and signify new life and growth. Rounded leaves are better than pointy ones. Avoid cacti, which create symbolic spears in your environment. Plants with flowers or fruit create more powerful cures. Fresh flowers will immediately uplift an environment. Dead vegetation is terrible energy — including any kind of dried flowers. Silk plants are a perfectly acceptable alternative to live ones, as silk is a natural fibre.

4. **Weight. Stones, rocks, boulders and statues are weight cures.**

- Stones, rocks and boulders can provide weight and stability to a space, creating calm.

- Symbolic statues can be used for weight — e.g., religious statues such as Buddha, Jesus, Virgin Mary, Angels, or animal statues such as elephants (for strength) or tortoises (for stability). Statues will also create calm.

5. **Colour.**

- Adding the correct colour to your home for that zone of the Bagua map will improve your home's energy enormously. You can paint the room or just add accents. You don't have to make each zone one colour only; you simply need to have items of the correct colour in the zone. Our bedroom is in our Prosperity zone, and we needed to add purple, but it didn't fit in with our colour scheme, so we lined all our drawers with purple paper. When adding colour cures you can add any shade of the colour, e.g., if you needed to add green to the Family zone, you could use a light mint green or a very dark hunter green, or any green in between. You can also change your personal Chi with the colour of the clothes that you are wearing. A favourite personal Chi adjustment is to wear red for nine days to increase personal power. I have red underwear for this occasion!

6.   Moving Objects.   Mobiles, windsocks and flags are moving cures.

- Mobiles add movement to a space and also help clear negative energy. They also soothe and create balance.

- Windsocks combine motion with colour and are especially effective at balancing Chi on the outside of a home.

- Flags can be used to add colour and lift the Chi.

  (Moving objects placed outside your home are covered in more detail in Section Five.)

7. **Electric Power.**

❷ The energy generated by a TV, computer, or fan can be used to create activity in the Children and Creativity or Helpful People and Travel zones. Rice cookers, slow cookers, etc. when placed on the kitchen counter stimulate the flow of money.

8. **Water. Fountains, water features, waterfalls and ponds are water cures.**

❷ Fountains and waterfalls create new energy. They bring money, peacefulness and harmony into the home.

❷ Indoor water has a refreshing impact on your home and a water feature with moving water symbolizes flowing money.

❷ Outdoor water gives a feeling of joy, life and beauty.

❷ Ponds represent stored wealth and depth of knowledge.

9. **Symbolic Objects. Bamboo flutes and red ribbons are symbolic cures.**

- Bamboo flutes are a most effective cure. Bamboo brings good luck and strength and provides support in your life. Bamboo also drives away negative energy. Flutes communicate peace and safety.

- When hanging crystal, chime, or mobiles use red ribbon. Red symbolizes fire and the energy that makes change happen. Cut your red ribbon in multiples of nine inches. Nine is the most powerful number in Feng Shui — the number of completion and accomplishment.

- Other cures can include personal and significant objects such as religious pictures or statues, or pictures of any hero of yours.

YOUR PERSONAL CHI ZONES

I have been talking a lot about the Chi of your environment and how to change your surroundings in order to be in the Feng Shui Zone. Part of being in this zone includes being aware of your personal Chi. Following is a wonderful exercise on how to be aware of your personal Chi (it was taught to me by another Feng Shui practitioner, but I don't know the original source). I call this your Personal Chi Zones.

Regardless of how many moods you have in a single day, there are only four states of personal Chi. It's a good idea to always know which of the four zones you are in at any given moment, so that you can adjust to circumstances quickly if you need to and keep or find your way to balance. The four Personal Chi Zones are:

CHI ZONES

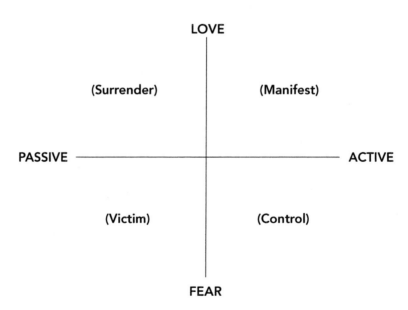

Are you in the love section, active or passive zones? Are you in the fear section, active or passive zones?

I'll give you an everyday example. You are sitting in traffic and a guy cuts you off and gives you the finger. You choose how you will react:

- If you're in the active fear zone you'll chase after him, honking and swearing. You, like the driver who cut you off, have become a controller.

- If you're in the passive fear zone you'll be weeping and wailing and feeling sorry for yourself thinking, Why does this always happen to me? You are now the victim.

- If you're in the passive love zone, you'll relax and say to yourself, I bet he has an emergency to go to. Here, you have allowed yourself to surrender.

- If you're in the active love zone you will act lovingly towards yourself and the other driver. Perhaps you left space for him to pull in front of you rather than squeezing him out in the first place.

EXERCISE: HOW TO BECOME AWARE OF YOUR PERSONAL CHI

The exercise is to keep the Personal Chi Zones in mind while you go through your day. Practise noticing each time you need to make a significant choice. Which Personal Chi Zone are you in? Do you wish to stay in this place? Are you ready to move from fear to love?

Knowledge is power and if you know which Personal Chi Zone you are in, you will know whether you need to adjust your Chi by changing your attitude. It often helps to take a time-out with a relaxing bath, using prayer, meditation or visualization or any other personal favourite that works for you. Remember that the Universe is abundant and will bring you everything you deserve.

4

Nine Steps to the Feng Shui Zone

Nine Steps to
the Feng Shui Zone

Being in the Feng Shui Zone means that your life will flow more smoothly and you will have greater life success. When your environmental Chi is balanced, your personal Chi will improve and this will increase the harmony and happiness in your life. In this section I will outline the nine steps to being in this zone. They are:

Step One: Setting Intentions
Step Two: Starting the Chi Flowing
Step Three: Clearing Outer Clutter
Step Four: Clearing Inner Clutter
Step Five: Personal Care

Step Six: Setting Personal Goals

Step Seven: Choosing Improvement

Step Eight: Applying Cures to Zones

Step Nine: Blessings

STEP ONE: SETTING INTENTIONS

I mentioned earlier that in BTB Feng Shui (the school we're following in this book) "intention" is a way to give power to your Feng Shui changes. The physical cure is said to influence the Chi by about 30 per cent, the other 70 per cent is influenced by your intention when doing the cure.

What is intention?

Intention is deciding what you want to achieve when you make the changes that will get you into the Feng Shui Zone. Why do you wish to use the power of Feng Shui? What areas of your life need help?

How do you set intentions?

Intention can be set through writing goals or using prayer, meditation, visualization, affirmation or any other spiritual tool. Meditation is a way to clear your mental clutter and visualization is a way to let the Universe know what it is you really hope to achieve in your life. Are you confident in the knowledge that the Universe is creative and that you can harness its power to work for you? Ask for what you want, express gratitude for what you know you are going to get and then have the quiet confidence that it will all be yours.

Before I start to apply cures to my own environment, I always set an intention. For example, I would consider what part of our life needs changing. Do we wish to improve our money situation, are we dealing with conflict in our family, are any of us unhappy with our careers or do our careers need a boost, do either of our sons need help with their studies or sports? First decide what you wish to change in your life and then begin your work on that zone in your environment.

STEP TWO: STARTING THE CHI FLOWING

The three most important areas of your home are the front door, your bed and the stove. Here are some key things to change to get the energy flowing in these areas.

Front Door. The front door represents the way life comes to you and is the Mouth of Chi.

- Clear the front door — there should be nothing around or behind it, and it must open easily, all the way. Keep it clean and make sure that it doesn't squeak. Remember this is your home's Mouth of Chi, this is how all the Chi enters your home. Quite an important job for a door, so give it the respect it deserves.

- Paint the front door red (or a shade of red — such as burgundy, rust, or cranberry) to protect your home and attract Chi. If this is not possible, place a red mat at the front door or hang a wreath (with predominantly red colours and NO dried flowers) on the front door.

- Place a water feature at the front door — inside or outside — to stimulate the flow of money and attract Chi.

- Hang wind chimes at the front door to attract Chi and disperse negative energy.

- Make sure the front door is well lit and very welcoming.

Bed and Bedroom. The bed shelters, comforts and enables true rest.

- Don't sleep on a used bed and never sleep on a bed from a previous relationship. A used or old bed carries baggage and negative Chi.

- The ideal size bed is a Queen size, whether you are in a relationship or not. King-sized beds create barriers; if you have one, place a red cloth beneath the mattress to add harmony to your relationship. Single beds will keep you alone as they have the Chi of "aloneness." Get yourself a Queen-sized bed to attract and keep someone special in your life.

- Waterbeds are not good, as they provide no firm foundation in life. Metal frame beds surround you in a magnetic field — not good for positive Chi. The ideal bed has a wooden bed base.

- Clear out under the bed — nothing should be stored underneath. Allow the Chi to circulate and you'll sleep better. Also, imagine what the Chi of all the stored stuff under the bed is doing to your peace and quiet. No wonder you're not sleeping well!

- An upholstered or wooden headboard provides stability and strength. I love this idea as it also provides the opportunity to introduce colour into the headboard. My favourites are red (for power and strength) and pink (for love).

- Nightstands should be equal in size and not too big and this will ensure an equal partnership.

- Try to place your bed in the "command" position in your bed-room. This is a position that will be mentioned quite a bit in this book. The best explanation that I have heard for this is the "Mafia" position. Imagine the mafia guy in a restaurant; he sits at the back of the room with his back to a solid wall; he has his bodyguards on either side of him; he can see the door and is completely pro-tected. Imagine the same position for your bed. Place the bed as far as possible from the bedroom door; be able to see most of the room from the bed; be able to see the bedroom door from the bed; and place the headboard along a solid wall. Also, don't have your feet or those of your partner facing directly out of the door when you're lying down. This is the death position! If you have an en suite bathroom, I have also found that it is not ideal to have your feet facing the bathroom door.

- You shouldn't be able to see yourself in any mirror when you are lying on your bed.

- Create a sacred space about you and your partner. Where do you want to go together, what are your goals and dreams? If you are looking for a relationship, use this space to show what you would like your future relationship to be — what kind of a person are you looking for, what interests would you like to share, etc.

- Get the computer, TV, ironing board, etc. out of the master bedroom. It is a place for sleep and for your personal relationship with both yourself and your partner.

- Parents should sleep in the master bedroom.

- Have one light that brightly lights the entire room by itself, or lamps of equal size on either side of the bed to encourage equality in the relationship.

- Hang a wind chime outside any bedroom door that leads to the exterior of your home, or hang a crystal inside any bedroom door that leads outside, to stop one partner from leaving the relationship.

- Align your drawers as they should be — socks at the bottom, underwear in the middle, sweaters at the top, etc. Jewellery and precious things should be placed in top drawers too.

- When choosing your sheet colours, red is for passion, pink is for love and romance, green is for money and new growth, yellow is for health and healing, purple is for abundance (not just financial prosperity), blue is for calm and relaxation, white is for communication.

Stove and Kitchen. This represents the source of your food and your ability to get enough food, as well as your abundance (not just your financial abundance).

- Clean the stove — inside and out. The stove has a profound effect on your prosperity and it should always be spotless. The stove represents your food and your ability to provide for your family.

- Make sure all the burners on the stove are in good working order and use each burner equally when you are cooking. We all have a favourite burner that we use more often, but it is important to use all of them equally.

- If your stove is against the wall — put a mirror behind it. This will reflect the food being cooked and double your wealth.

- If the sink or dishwasher is opposite the stove, fire and water are in conflict and you should place wood between them, for example a green-coloured mat or a plant.

- If the fridge and stove are side-by-side, fire and water are in conflict and once again you should place wood between them — green poster board slipped between them will work as it is the colour of wood and the paper also is made of wood pulp.

- If a bathroom is above or below the kitchen, fire and water are in conflict. The ceiling between the two needs to be painted green (wood element). Or you could simply place a large green mat on the floor of the room above.

- Hang a crystal above the microwave oven to absorb its negative energy.

Here are some changes that need to be made in other areas of your home.

Dining Room.

- Hang a large mirror to reflect the food on the table — to double your food wealth.

- Stop eating in the kitchen, living room, bedroom, etc.; eat in the dining room at least once a day. The dining room is a very important room in your home as it impacts your prosperity.

Bathrooms.

Bathrooms are "tricky" rooms in the home. Apply cures to stop your money from going down the drain.

- Put plants in the bathrooms — real or silk. We know that the Five Elements interact with each other and the Earth element dams Water (the earth in the pot of the plant) and Water feeds Wood (the plant itself). A plant in the bathroom will help balance the effect of too much Water element.

- Keep your toilet seats down and the bathroom doors closed at all times. This is tough if there are men in the house, but it can be done with a little persistence. My teenaged boys soon got tired of being asked to put the seat down, especially when they were in the basement busy with their friends. They do it automatically now and we've almost got all their friends on track too!

Living Room.

- The seating should be arranged so that everyone sitting in the living room can see the main entrance or door. Once again, we're looking for the "command position" to provide everyone who sits in the living room with a sense of security and protection.

❷ Place the furniture in a conversational way, closer together rather than around the walls. A good "rule of thumb" is each person should be able to touch the person in the next chair when sitting down.

Drains.

❷ Stop your Chi and your money from literally going down your drains! Put red tape around all drainpipes leaving the house — sinks, toilets, washing machine, etc.

❷ Place a red line along the floor at the entrance to all the bathrooms. I used red electrical tape, but I have seen red nail varnish used too. One client lifted up the strip on the floor at the entrance to her bathrooms and placed red tape beneath it.

❷ Attach three-inch convex mirrors (the ones sold for Recreational Vehicles that attach to the wing mirrors) near or below all drain pipes leaving your home. For the shower and tub, stick one on the side of the shower/tub in line with the drain hole; for the drain pipes out of the basin in the bathroom and the sink in the kitchen you can place the mirror directly below the "U" in the pipe beneath the sink; for the toilet, place the convex mirror directly behind the toilet on the floor; for the washing machine, place the convex mirror as close to the grey-water outlet as possible. The dishwasher usually drains out of the same pipe as the kitchen sink, so the convex mirror below the "U" under the kitchen sink will work for it too.

Mirrors.

- Hang a mirror above the fireplace. Fireplaces have very strong fire energy and the mirror (water) will balance it. Too much fire energy can cause arguments in the family.

- All mirrors should be hung so that they don't cut off the head of the tallest person in the family when they are standing looking into it.

Books.

- Move all your books to be lined up with the front of your bookshelves as this will stop the dust and dirt accumulating on the shelves in front of them.

- Put your sacred or inspirational books on the top shelf. This shows respect and places them where they should be.

Crystals.

Crystals are usually 30 mm (1") in size; they should be an even round shape and should ideally be hung using nine inches of red ribbon. Clear-coloured crystals are excellent, but if you prefer the coloured ones (blue, green, pink, red) you could choose the correct colour for that zone of your home, depending on where you are going to hang them.

- Hang crystals in front of all sliding doors.

- Hang a crystal in the middle of each bedroom.

- Hang crystals from ceiling fans. You can actually get fan chain pulls with crystals at the end.

- Hang a crystal in any windowless room.

- Hang a crystal in front of any bedroom door that leads to the exterior of your house.

- Hang a crystal from the ceiling directly over the position of your head when sitting in your office or study chair.

Lighting.

- Add light to the interior and exterior entranceway to your home, as this will increase the Chi in this very important area.

- All important rooms — bedroom, kitchen and dining room — should have bright lights.

- Make sure each room is lit equally on both sides.

Other.

- Check all your artwork for symbolism. Make sure all the pictures on your walls have uplifting images — things that make you feel good when you look at them. Take down all photos of previously unhappy times.

- TVs should ideally be placed inside cabinets, but if this is not possible, place plants around the TV to absorb negative energy, three if there is room.

- Make sure all the drawers in your furniture slide smoothly.

Your next step will be to thoroughly de-clutter your home. Improvements to the energy in your surroundings will improve your personal Chi and cause change for the better in all areas of your life. Simple, isn't it?

STEP THREE: CLEARING OUTER CLUTTER

Clearing clutter is a wonderful part of applying Feng Shui techniques, both the outer clutter (those overstuffed closets) and the inner clutter (all those negative thoughts). My good friend once said of clutter, "Tidying a kitchen drawer gives me a good feeling every time I walk past it, even if I don't open the drawer." She was able to feel the good Chi. Imagine how your entire home could make you feel!

The Benefits of Clearing Clutter

Because we know that making changes to the energy in your surroundings affects your personal energy, it naturally follows that clearing your outer clutter will stimulate those internal energy changes and improve your life success. Everything around you (including your clutter and mess) mirrors your inner self and your home is a reflection of your life. Removing obstacles to a smooth, free flow of Chi in your home improves your personal Chi, creates harmony in your life and makes space for exciting opportunities. Clearing clutter can improve your relationships, your health and your flow of finances.

Negative Effects of Clutter

The problem with accumulated clutter is that it weighs you down literally and figuratively, plus clutter stops the flow of Chi and has an unpleasant energy. If you clear your clutter you will increase the energy flow in your surroundings, and you'll feel better because your personal Chi will enjoy an energy boost too. If energy is stagnant, clutter will accumulate and the more clutter you have the more it attracts stagnant energy. Things just keep going from bad to worse. Have you noticed how mess gathers around mess? How a few things left lying around easily becomes a big pile of stuff? A space filled with unnecessary things slows down your life, making it harder to progress and move forward.

The Reasons why we Clutter

Clutter has nothing to do with a lack of self-control or being a bad person. Clutter is an outward manifestation of our inner life. The "stuff" in your life isn't the problem; the "stuff" in your head is the problem.

Since all aspects of our self are inter related, when we shift our physical environment (by clearing clutter) we will also be moved emotionally, mentally, spiritually. Clutter is tangible, which makes it an easy place to go to work on our life. It is one aspect that we can actually get our hands on. We clear ourselves of negative thinking when we clear out our clutter.

Our clutter is our security blanket — we are either exactly like or exactly opposite what we learn as children. We don't throw things away because we don't want to be alone. We don't throw things away because we're afraid of losing love. Clutter affects our personality — it makes us shy, fearful, angry and feeds our low self esteem. We need to get rid of the excuses: "I'm an artist. Artists are messy." "I am a genius. Einstein was a clutterer." "I am ...., it's part of our culture."

> *Having too much stuff keeps wealth*
> *from flowing into your life.*
>
> Suze Orman

Cluttered or Not-so-cluttered?

Each of us has a personal comfort zone about clutter. What might be considered clutter by a "metal" person wouldn't even make the radar screen of an "earth" person. Look at your home and make an objective assessment of the amount of stuff lying around. (For a quick guide to finding out what your element is, refer to *Feng Shui Your Kitchen* by Sharon Stasney.)

Clutter-clearing Strategies

If you don't love it or absolutely need it, throw it out. Things that are loved and used have a strong, clear, free-flowing energy around them. If you surround yourself with things that have this free-flowing energy, you will have a loving, useful and happy life. On the other hand, anything unused, unloved, neglected or forgotten will cause your personal energy to slow down and stagnate; you will feel that your life is not moving. If you store too much stuff (for a rainy day!) energy can't flow.

Steps to Clearing your Clutter

Just to make it a bit easier, I have set down a work plan for clearing your clutter. If you follow these steps you will free up the Chi and improve your life success.

- Make a conscious decision to keep fewer material things. This will keep the Chi flowing in your home, office, car and attract new prosperity.

- Work on the 50:50 rule. All surfaces should never be more than half covered with things, all drawers should only be filled 50 per cent. This allows room for new opportunities to enter your life.

- Start clearing clutter in the zone that relates to the area of your life that needs most work (refer to the Bagua map in Section Three).

- Set aside a regular time to de-clutter, for example, once a week. If possible work with a partner or friend.

- Plan your de-cluttering, think about the areas that need clearing and set goals for each week.

- Set up four boxes for clearing — one for donations, one for throwing out, one for giving to family or friends and one for your garage sale. Get rid of the clutter as soon as possible. Make the trip to the dump and charity the same day. I had a client whose china cabinet was filled to bursting with a huge tea set that belonged to her late husband's family. She wasn't particularly attached to the tea set and decided to give it to one of her husband's nieces. The niece was thrilled, my client got the tea set out of her cabinet, making room for her other china, and everyone was happy.

- Clean each area as you remove the clutter. Chi cannot flow through a dirty and dusty area. Don't forget the windows as you clean each area. Clean both the inside and outside of the windows. Make sure that there are no obstructions in front of them — furniture on the inside and trees and bushes on the outside.

- Add aromatherapy oils to the area once it is cleaned and clutter free. Simply add a few drops to the furniture in the area, but remember that it is oil so don't put it anywhere that it could stain. Aromatherapy oils that work really well for cleaning and de-cluttering are pine, lemongrass, rosemary and citronella.

- Fix things as you move from room to room clearing and cleaning. Remember to replace those broken light bulbs.

- Replace all the trashcans in your home with ones with lids. Don't allow your Chi to go into the garbage.

- Throw out all dried flowers and weak, unhealthy plants and trees, etc. This includes your potpourri — it has dead Chi. Can you think of any more negative energy than that?

◑ Hang a crystal in the Skills and Knowledge (bottom left) zone of your home to help you become neater and cleaner.

In our home we started clearing clutter from closets and once we'd cleared them once, we went through them again. It's absolutely amazing how much you'll clear out a second or even a third time around.

Making Your Home Clutter-free, Room by Room
Because clutter can be such a big issue with many people, I have laid out a few practical ways to clear clutter, focusing on some key areas of your environment. Find what works for you though — everyone has their own way to deal with clearing and sorting.

Bedroom. Don't keep things in the bedroom that don't belong there, like the TV. Bedrooms are for sleeping and for your relationship, nothing else. Your bed shelters, comforts and enables you to get true rest. Stale energy hangs around dirty laundry too, so change your bed sheets often to keep your own energy fresh.

Front door. All of the energy that enters your home enters through this door. The front door is your home's Mouth of Chi. If this area is cluttered in any way it can restrict the flow of opportunities into your life. Clutter in this area causes struggle in your life.

From the outside, take a long hard look at your front door. Are there any overhanging branches or plants blocking it? Is there junk anywhere around it? Does anything hinder your walking into or out of it? From the inside, are there coats, shoes, or furniture in your way? Does the door open freely all the way? ALL THE WAY? Give this door a regular cleaning — wash down both the outside and inside, wipe off the door knob, make sure all mechanics work smoothly.

Kitchen. Don't collect old food in your cupboards. Have a major clear-out, including the fridge and freezer. Go through all the drawers and clear out kitchen items you haven't used in a while; also, you don't really need to keep duplicates. Go through all your cupboards, keep what you love and need and put the rest aside for a garage sale or for donation to a worthy cause. Clean the stove inside and out — it is a reflection of your prosperity. A dirty stove — poor prosperity!

Back door. If you don't want your home to be clogged, clear the clutter from the back door too.

Behind doors. Clear the clutter from behind all the doors in your home, including things hanging from hooks and doorknobs. Make sure all doors can open without any obstructions. This is a simple and effective way of getting the energy to flow freely in your home. You'll notice how much easier your life becomes — as the Chi flows more easily, your life moves more easily too.

Passageways. Keep all these areas as clear as possible. Don't allow anything to get in your way as you move down the passage, as this will also obstruct the flow of energy. Remove any furniture that obstructs your path — it will slow down the Chi too.

Wardrobe. Don't keep any clothes that you haven't worn in the past year. Keep only clothes that you love to wear, things that make you feel good. Throw out all your "I-wish-I-were-thinner" clothes because keeping your closet stuffed with clothes you don't wear doesn't leave room for any wonderful new clothes.

Bathroom. A bathroom filled with products, appliances and junk is hard to clean. Your bathroom should be peaceful and calm and needs to be clutter free. Keep your bathroom drawers and cupboards organized and throw out all those empty bottles. Bring in candles, fragrances and relaxing music.

Garage. Only keep things you use and like in your garage. A clean, well-organized space will enable the energy to flow freely. Be disciplined in this area of your home, as it is the easiest place to put things "just in case." Make sure that the garage is well lit and the garage door lubed and not squeaky.

Car. Keep your car clean and clutter-free. Clear out all the mess and garbage and you'll enjoy a release of energy. Driving in a clean car will energize you and make you a better driver.

Purses, briefcases, backpacks. Don't carry your clutter around with you as you'll just be blocking your Chi everywhere you go. Clean out these items often — especially all those bits of paper. Hang a 20-mm (¾") crystal on any of these items to take clarity and good energy everywhere you go.

You have accomplished the satisfying task of de-cluttering your home — congratulations. Remember it's not cleaning, it's getting your life into the Feng Shui Zone. Check your personal Chi. Do you need a relaxing bath to recover from the exhaustion of moving all this energy? (More on personal care in Step Five.)

STEP FOUR: CLEARING INNER CLUTTER

Now that you have started to deal with the clutter in your home and environment, it is time to start working on the "inner" clutter. Clearing the clutter in your mind is just as important as clearing the clutter in your living space. Wouldn't you feel great if you could get rid of all those negative thoughts that swirl around your brain all day? You can, if you learn to meditate and visualize and make time to do that at least three times a week for twenty minutes. That's all it takes!

Benefits of a Clutter-free Mind

Our minds create our thoughts and beliefs, and the key to abundant and happy living is belief. Whatever you believe to be true is true. If you think poverty, you will be poor; if you think wealth, it will be yours.

Also, every thought has energy — so negative thoughts give you negative energy; positive thoughts give you positive energy. That is the law of the Universe. The wonderful teacher, Dr. Wayne Dyer, teaches that you get back from the Universe what you put into it. So if you put out that you are not worthy, you will get back that you are not worthy. If you say to the Universe, "How may I serve you?" the Universe will say back, "How may I serve YOU?"

Do you realize that you have a subconscious mind of limitless power and potential and that your mind is connected to the immense power of the Universe? Do you accept the truth that your mind has the capacity to make whatever you wish come true, and nothing is impossible? If you accept the power of your subconscious mind as reality, you will be on your way to having everything you really want.

The mind is everything,
what you think you become.

Buddha

Sitting Meditation

There are many forms of meditation that have been practised for thousands of years. These practices use breath, and a mantra (sound) and a mudra (hand position) to reach a place of stillness within. The purpose is to either go to a place beyond the mind; or to learn how to not attach to the thoughts passing through the mind. There are many resources available to learn how to meditate. My favourite, *Inner and Outer Peace through Meditation*, by Rajinder Singh, is listed in the Resources section.

Guided Meditation or Visualization

For some people, it is easier to move beyond negative thoughts and de-clutter the mind by using guided meditations or visualizations. Visualizations use your imagination to create visions of success. They are a guided tour through a series of thoughts that will help change your negative thoughts and instill a successful belief system. For an incredible guide to visualization, read *The Secrets of Creative Visualization* by Philip Cooper.

Over the years I have taught and studied many different meditations and visualizations and in the Resources section you will find some of my favourites. These visualizations have all been modified from ones given by my teachers and found in the books that I have studied. In some instances I do not know from whom they originated, and in some instances they are of my own design.

STEP FIVE: PERSONAL CARE

Now, perhaps more than at any other time in our evolution, we need to be clear and aware of the problems that beset us, but our endeavours become pointless unless we appreciate that we have become masters of our own destiny. We need to know where we are going and how we are going to get there. Already we have begun to make use of our conscious talents, but we have completely neglected those available on the other side of the mind. Nature has given us all the necessary equipment for our task in the space between our ears ... All that remains is for us to use them wisely.

Lyall Watson, *Supernature*, p. 244

There are a number of things you can do to take care of yourself, which is taking care of your personal Chi. You may find that as you move into the Feng Shui Zone you become more sensitive and aware of this need to care for yourself. Here are some tools that I use to care for myself.

Heart Calming Meditation

One of the meditations that I use most often is the Heart Calming Meditation. If you need a personal Chi adjustment, you're having a tough day or anticipate a difficult meeting (actually for any reason), draw upon thousands of years of universal teaching to calm your heart and mind. This meditation can also be used first thing in the morning or last thing at night to quiet your mind and connect you with the creative and generous Universe.

Place your left hand on top of your right hand, palms up, thumbs touching, in front of your chest. Recite the heart-

calming mantra. Gate, gate, para gate, para sum gate, bodhi swa ha (pronounced gatay, gatay, para gatay, para soom gatay, bowdhee swa ha). The literal translation of these sacred words is "gone, gone, gone across, completely gone across, the enlightened state, it is accomplished, I recognize this truth in myself." Think about your heart and mind growing calmer and more peaceful and connect with the Universe. Repeat the words nine times.

Relaxing Bath Cures

Another great way to adjust your personal Chi is to take a relaxing bath cure at least once a week. I know you can make the time! Set up your bathroom with candles, essential oil burners, creams and lotions and a thick comfortable bathrobe. While you are bathing either meditate or listen to relaxing music.

Following are examples of additional bath cures you may want to use:

1.   To clear your energy field — use this bath if you have been in crowds of people, work with the public or have had contact with negative or sick people.

a.   Bathe in 1 cup of sea salt, 1 cup of baking soda, 3 capfuls of hydrogen peroxide (food strength). Drink a glass of spring water before, during and after the bath. Have a shower afterwards.

b.   Wash and peel nine oranges. Put the peels in the bathtub with 1 lb of sea salt. Drink a glass of spring water before, during and after the bath. Have a shower afterwards.

2.   When you're feeling sick — this cure works equally well for sickness or injury.

Bathe in 1 cup sea salt, 1 cup baking soda, 3 tablespoons ground ginger. Drink a glass of spring water before, during and after the bath. Have a shower afterwards.

3.   Aromatherapy oils produce positive physiological and psychological effects and when they are combined, the effects of the individual oils are magnified. Add 5 drops to your bath, just before you get in.

Try these blends:

To relieve stress, blend 3 drops lavender and 2 drops ylang ylang.

To uplift your mood, try 3 drops bergamot and 2 drops geranium.

For when you're not feeling well, add 3 drops marjoram and 2 drops chamomile.

STEP SIX: SETTING PERSONAL GOALS

The truth is that as much as you plan and dream and move forward in your life, you must remember you are always acting in conjunction with the flow and energy of the Universe. You move in the direction of your goal with all the force and verve you can muster — and then let go, releasing your plan to the power that's bigger than yourself and allowing your dream to unfold as its own masterpiece. Dream big — dream very big. Work hard — work very hard. And after you've done all you can, you stand, wait, and fully surrender.

Oprah Winfrey

Goals are the specifics of where you want to go with your life. It is essential to write your goals down and I recommend that you read them every day. Write a goal for each zone of your life: one for abundance and prosperity (Prosperity Zone), one for recognition and standing in the community (Fame Zone), one for your special relationships (Relationships and Love Zone), one for each of your children and your creative talents (Creativity and Children Zone), one for your travel plans and volunteer efforts (Helpful People and Travel Zone), one for your career (Career and Life Path Zone), one for your studies and Spiritual development (Skills and Knowledge Zone), one for your family (Family Zone), one for your health (Health Zone).

Here are some tips for writing goals that will work:

- Visualize your goals.

- Be specific. Engage all of your five senses: sight, touch, smell, sound and taste. Know what you want.

- Express your goals in the positive.

◉ Express your goals as if they have already been achieved. Focus your attention on the result.

◉ Expect and believe that the results will happen.

◉ Let go of your plan.

For example, if being healthy is your intention, here is a sample of a "health" goal: "I am moving freely as I go about my daily business. I am free of back pain. I feel very light and my skin enjoys being touched. I am able to walk in the beautiful sunshine to my favourite coffee shop for a delicious latte. I am enjoying the birds and the fresh air as I spend more time outdoors and am filled with the smell of nature."

STEP SEVEN: CHOOSING IMPROVEMENT

Look well of today — for it is the Life of Life. In its brief course lie all the variations and realities of your life — the bliss of growth, the glory of action, the splendour of beauty. For yesterday is but a dream, and tomorrow a vision. But today well-lived makes every yesterday a dream of happiness, and every tomorrow a vision of hope. For time is but a scene in the eternal drama. So, look well of today, and let that be your resolution as you awake each morning and salute the New Dawn. Each day is born by the recurring miracle of Dawn, and each night reveals the celestial harmony of the stars.

M. Wylie Blanchet, *The Curve of Time*, p. 62

Which area of your life do you wish to improve? There may be a part of your life that needs a complete change, a part that needs a little enhancement, something happening in the lives of your loved ones. Up to now you have prepared yourself and your home for Feng Shui by cleaning, clearing and fixing. You have learned about the Bagua map and how to apply it to your home. You have learned about some of the cures and tried them out also. The next step to improving the Chi in your home and life is to focus on one aspect of your life you want to improve. Is it Prosperity? Fame? Relationships and Love? Creativity and

Children? Helpful People and Travel? Career and Life Path? Skills and Knowledge? Family? Health?

Perhaps you feel several aspects need improvement. How do you choose just one? Just choose a place to start according to your most urgent need and then move onto the other zones. Once you have chosen your focus, check where that zone of the Bagua map is located in your home. For example, Prosperity is in the back left corner. Start to apply the techniques of Feng Shui by clearing out the clutter and cleaning thoroughly, and then follow Step Eight.

STEP EIGHT: APPLYING CURES TO ZONES

Remember that cures are remedies for your energy problems and the Bagua is the map showing how and where to apply the cures. Here are some other reminders about the Bagua map:

- The best way to lay the Bagua map is using a floor plan. Place the Bagua map on your floor plan and then walk around your home and make a mental note of which rooms correspond to which zones.

- ❧ You can lay the Bagua map over your entire home, and over each room.

- ❧ Don't divide rooms into two zones if possible. What I mean is, if the bedroom overlaps Prosperity and Fame, but is mostly in Prosperity, then "intend" that this room be in the Prosperity zone.

- ❧ Be aware that some of the zone cures take place outside of the area. For example, many of the Relationship and Love zone changes happen in the master bedroom, regardless of which zone the master bedroom falls into.

In this step, you get to put into practice what you have learned so far, using your focus. Each zone is described and an action plan is provided. Once again, don't forget to keep a record of the changes you are making and the impact they are having on your life success.

PROSPERITY ZONE

Every man is the architect of his own fortune.

Sallust

Zone Details

- Location — Back upper left zone
- Element — Wood
- Characteristics — Expansive, growing, flexible, tough, creating
- Colours — Purple, green, red

This zone on the Bagua map corresponds to your abundance — abundant money, abundant health and all of your other blessings. Zone in here and some of the wonderful results will be that you will make more money, increase money for whatever you want to do, increase the happiness and abundance in your life and find inner peace.

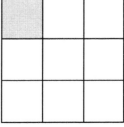

PROSPERITY ZONE

Zone Action Plan

The action lists are not dependent on what room falls into the zone. Remember that some changes need to take place outside of the area, which in this case is the back upper left of your home.

- Check your Bagua map and you will see that you need to add the colours purple, red or green.

- Introduce things that remind you of abundance — gold nuggets, pictures of expensive cars or homes etc. Use your imagination. A client of mine framed money and hung it on the wall in this zone.

- Add moving water (this is a wood zone and water feeds wood).

- Add healthy plants (or silk if you prefer).

- Clean this zone very well. No dust, dirt or clutter.

- Remove all broken and chipped items.

- Replace all garbage cans with ones with lids on.

- Fill the refrigerator with fresh and healthy foods.

- Keep a bowl filled with fresh fruit and vegetables on the kitchen counter.

- Remove all storage items from this area, e.g., old income tax files, old documents.

- Keep the toilet seat down in all bathrooms and keep the bathroom doors closed at all times.

- Repair all leaky faucets and blocked drains.

- Place all sharp knives in a kitchen drawer or cupboard, even if you use a knife block. Don't leave them on the counter.

- Keep all areas of your home well lit, particularly this zone.

- Volunteer more — remember you get back from the Universe what you put into it.

- Clean your stove inside and out and keep it very clean. Make sure it is in good working order.

- Place a mirror behind the stove to reflect the burners and double your prosperity.

- Ensure that you use all four burners equally.

- Hang a large mirror to reflect the food on the dining-room table — to double your food wealth.

- Stop eating in the kitchen and start eating in the dining room. The dining room impacts your prosperity and is therefore a very important room in your home.

- Stop your money from literally going down the drain:
    - Red tape around all drain pipes leaving your home
    - Red line along the entrance floor to the bathrooms
    - Convex mirrors below/beside all drains (refer to Step Two).

FAME ZONE

What we steadily, consciously, habitually think we
are, that we tend to become.

Ann Landers

Zone Details

- Location — Back upper central zone
- Element — Fire
- Characteristics — Hot, explosive, enlightened, clear, bright
- Colours — Red

This zone on the Bagua map corresponds to how you see yourself and how others see you. Zone in here and you will improve your reputation, improve business, gain courage to do whatever you want to do, gain respect from others, and become well-known. You will be able to set goals and plan your future.

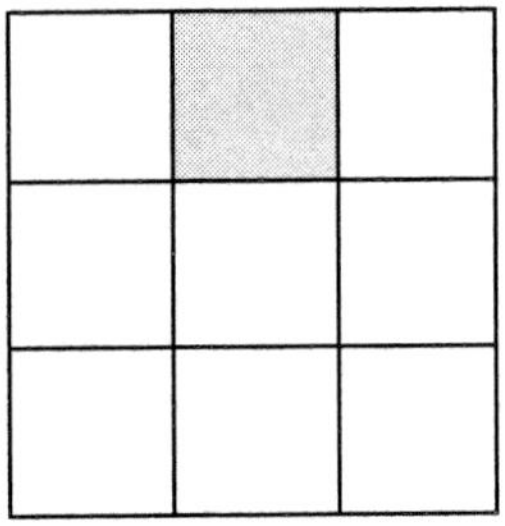

FAME ZONE

Zone Action Plan

- Add red items and fire (candles, pictures of sunsets, etc.) to this zone.

- Hang pictures or memorabilia of people that you admire.

- This is a great place to hang your awards or diplomas.

- Remove any water from this area (water destroys fire).

- Make sure that all your windows and mirrors are clean and crack-free.

- Have at least one mirror in each room of your home.

- This is the best place in your home for a fireplace and the best place on your deck for the barbecue or fire pit.

- Keep this area well lit.

- Write your goals and read them every day.

RELATIONSHIPS AND LOVE ZONE

We can only learn to love by loving.

Doris Murdock

Zone Details

- ☯ Location — Back upper right zone
- ☯ Element — Earth
- ☯ Characteristics — Firm, reliable, receptive, nourishing, romantic
- ☯ Colours — Pink, red, white

This zone on the Bagua map corresponds to your relationship with your partner and most importantly, yourself. Zone in here and you will find a significant other (if you are looking), or improve your existing relationship.

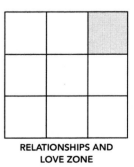

**RELATIONSHIPS AND
LOVE ZONE**

Zone Action Plan

Regardless of which zone your bedroom falls into, it plays a huge part in the energy of your relationships and the changes listed below are for the Relationship and Love zone as well as for the master bedroom. If your bedroom happens to fall into the Relationship and Love zone you are very lucky, but don't worry if it doesn't, as once you have implemented these cures below you will boost your relationship to a higher level!

- Add a mirror to this zone — actually you should aim to have a mirror in each room of your home. Remember, in your bedroom you shouldn't see yourself in the mirror when you are lying on your bed.

- Introduce candles, fresh or silk flowers and yin textiles (luxurious, soft, sensual) to the master bedroom.

- Add pink or red colours to this zone.

- Stand at your bedroom door. Notice the objects you have placed in the relationship zone — the far right corner of the room. Create a "couple" display in this part of the bedroom. This could be of your existing relationship (if you are in one) or of a relationship you are hoping to start.

- Place your bed in the "command" position in your bedroom. Place the bed as far as possible from the bedroom door. Be able to see most of the room and the bedroom door from the bed. Place the headboard along a solid wall. Don't have your feet, or those of your partner, facing directly out of the door when you're lying down (this is the position of death!).

- Remove all dead/dried flowers and plants from your entire home, including the potpourri.

- Place items in your bedroom that have special significance to you and your (existing or potential) partner, e.g., painting of a couple, two beautiful plants, romantic memorabilia.

- Remove all items that represent something single, e.g., any single item — one candle (add another to make a pair), one lonely statue, and pictures of when you were single, etc.

- Place recent photos of you and your partner in the relationship area of your bedroom and other main rooms in your home.

- Make sure that the night tables and lamps on either side of the bed are the same size and prominence. This will ensure balance in the relationship.

- Only have books and music that are loved and encourage personal growth in your bedroom. Avoid negative subjects.

- Create a Yin bedroom — soft plush textiles, sheets of the highest quality.

- Put red and pink sheets on your bed, for love and passion.

- Remove the computer, TV, ironing board, etc., from the bedroom. This is a place for you and your partner.

- Hang a wind chime outside any bedroom door that leads to the outside of your home; or a crystal inside this bedroom door.

- Have one light in the center of the room that brightly lights the entire room by itself.

- Parents must sleep in the master bedroom.

- Remember these rules for your bed referred to in Section Two:
    - The ideal bed size is Queen size
    - Don't sleep on a used bed or one from a previous relationship
    - If the bed is King size, place a red cloth beneath the mattress
    - Store nothing under the bed
    - Sleep on a wooden bed with a solid headboard

CREATIVITY AND CHILDREN ZONE

In the long run, men hit only what they aim at.
Therefore, though they should fail immediately,
they had better aim at something high.

Henry David Thoreau

Zone Details

- ◉ Location   Middle right central zone
- ◉ Element   Metal
- ◉ Characteristics   Contracting, heavy, creative
- ◉ Colours   White

This zone on the Bagua map represents your children, creativity, happiness and potential. Zone in here and you will find fulfillment with your job and hobby, improve your relationship with your children, improve the health and well-being of your children, increase your creativity, become more relaxed and improve your communication skills.

**CREATIVITY AND
CHILDREN ZONE**

Zone Action Plan

- Add white and metal items to this zone.

- This is a great place for the TV and computer. If that is not possible, place the TV and computer in this zone of the room they are in.

- Set up an area in this zone for your hobbies and crafts. Relocate your art studio, writing area, sewing machine, etc., to this zone.

- Hang a mirror over the fireplace.

- Remove all candles and red items from this zone.

- Make sure that all drawers open easily and smoothly all over the house.

- Place stuffed animals or things that remind you of children in this zone.

- Place inspiring items on the walls of this zone to get the creative juices flowing.

- Keep your cookbooks, art books and craft books here.

HELPFUL PEOPLE AND TRAVEL ZONE

The fragrance always stays in the hand that gives the rose.

Hada Bejar

Zone Details

- Location — Right zone of entrance wall
- Element — Metal
- Characteristics — Contracting, heavy, energetic
- Colours — Grey, black, white

This zone on the Bagua map represents all those people who are helpful to us, as well as our travel plans. It is my experience that the quickest and most noticeable changes happen when you make energy-enhancement changes here. You will find helpful people when you need them, find yourself in the right place at the right time, find the right people to help you and teach you, give more of yourself as you receive more, travel more and your travelling will become easier.

**HELPFUL PEOPLE AND
TRAVEL ZONE**

Zone Action Plan

- Add the colours silver and grey to this zone.

- Introduce symbols of helpful beings — angels, Virgin Mary, Buddha, or people who are helpful to you, like your grandmother.

- Display "helping hands," any picture or ornament of hands.

- Add water to this zone. This could be a small water feature, picture of water or a mirror.

- Look for opportunities to help other people.

- Place pictures or magazines of places you would like to visit in this zone.

- Display silver items here — keep them clean and polished.

- Remove any reminders of financial bad times.

- Karen Rauch Carter, author of *Move Your Stuff, Change Your Life*, suggests keeping the names of three people from whom you need help in a silver container. Keep this updated as your needs change.

CAREER AND LIFE PATH ZONE

Do not fear going forward slowly; fear only standing still.

Chinese Proverb

Zone Details

- Location — Front centre of entrance wall
- Element — Water
- Characteristics — Fluid, reflective, deep, still, thoughtful
- Colours — Black, dark blue

This zone on the Bagua map corresponds to your career and your life's passion. Zone in here and you will get a more meaningful job, enjoy your work more, make more money in your business, or find out what you want to do with your life.

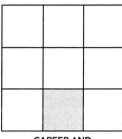

**CAREER AND
LIFE PATH ZONE**

Zone Action Plan

- Add the colour black to this zone.

- Introduce water at the front door — inside or outside.

- Add symbols of the life you want to have, e.g., pictures, books.

- Make sure that the front door to your home doesn't stick and that there is nothing cluttered around it.

- Make sure that the door to your office opens easily, doesn't stick at all.

- Make an effort to use the front door to your home (even if another door is more convenient). Not using the front door causes energy to stagnate.

- Make sure the doorbell works and that the entrance is well lit.

- Paint the front door red or an acceptable shade of red such as burgundy, rust, cranberry. If this is not possible, place a red door-mat at the front door or a wreath with flowers and ribbons that are predominantly red. (Remember no dried flowers in the wreath.) Wash the front door often.

- Hang a mirror in the entrance hall to draw energy into your home.

- Hang a wind chime outside the front door to attract Chi into the home.

SKILLS AND KNOWLEDGE ZONE

Live as if you were to die tomorrow.

Learn as if you were to live forever.

Mahatma Gandhi

Zone Details

⊘	Location	Left zone of entrance wall
⊘	Element	Earth
⊘	Characteristics	Careful, still, stable, reliable
⊘	Colours	Blue, green, black

This zone on the Bagua map represents knowledge, wisdom and spiritual development. Zone in here and you will get better grades, become a better business person, attract new opportunities, find inner wisdom and grow spiritually.

**SKILLS AND
KNOWLEDGE ZONE**

Zone Action Plan

- Add the colour blue to this zone.

- Keep your meditation or religious items here.

- This is a great place for your symbols of mentors and wise people such as your spiritual leader, favourite teacher.

- Spend time each week nurturing and cultivating yourself. Take a "relaxing bath cure" once a week.

- Find an area in your home solely for quiet time. Make this a sacred place for being at peace.

- Learn to meditate and practice visualization. Meditate at least three times per week, for 20 minutes at a time. (Refer to the Resources section.)

- Clear out this zone, remove clutter and keep it well organized.

- Start a regular exercise program.

- Put a bookcase filled with inspirational books in this area.

- Remove all alcohol, drugs (medications) from this zone.

- Remove newspapers — they are filled with unwise people and bad news.

- Clear out the garage; lube the door; add light; clean the cars — even if the garage is not in this zone.

FAMILY ZONE

Where there is love, there is life.

Mahatma Gandhi

Zone Details

- Location   Middle left central zone
- Element   Wood
- Characteristics   Upward movement, expansive, energetic, determined
- Colours   Green, blue

This zone on the Bagua map represents family, close friends and co-workers. Zone in here and you will build stronger relationships with family, friends and co-workers, improve harmony in your home, resolve conflicts, build your confidence to meet life's challenges, stabilize family finances and have enough money to pay the family bills.

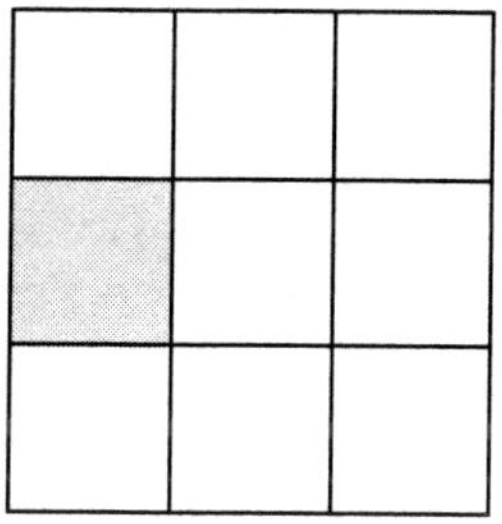

FAMILY ZONE

Zone Action Plan

- Add the colour green to this zone.

- Introduce water here (water feeds wood), e.g., a water feature, mirror.

- Place three, six or nine real or silk plants in this zone.

- Hang pictures of your family showing happy times.

- Place books, games and cards in this area to encourage interaction.

- Plan recreation times with family and close friends.

- Position furniture so that conversation is easy — don't put chairs along the wall and in corners of rooms. A good rule of thumb is that you should be able to reach out and touch the person in the next chair.

- Remove guns from this area. Not just real guns, but pictures too.

- Hang a crystal in any windowless room.

- Enclose the TV in a cabinet, or place plants around the TV. (Place the TV in the Children and Creativity or Helpful people and Travel zones of the room.)

HEALTH ZONE

You, yourself, as much as anybody in the entire
Universe, deserve your love and affection.

Buddha

Zone Details

- Location   Middle zone of your home
- Element   Earth
- Characteristics   Firm, stable, reliable, still, growing
- Colours   Yellow, earth tones

This zone on the Bagua map represents overall health, both physical and mental, and balance in the Universe. Zone in here and you will improve your health, improve your state of mind, increase a sense of balance in your life, and increase your energy.

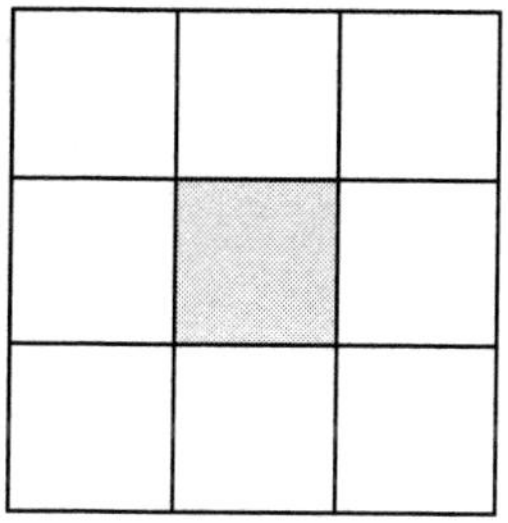

HEALTH ZONE

Zone Action Plan

- Add earth tones to this area — yellow, gold, peach, etc.

- Add items made from the earth such as pottery, ceramics.

- Keep this area clean and clutter-free.

- Remove all old, broken, unused items from this zone.

- Hang a 40-mm (1 ½") crystal in this zone, or add a crystal light or chandelier.

- Integrate all Five Elements — wood, fire, metal, water, earth — for balance.

- Place symbols of good health in this zone such as fresh fruit, exercise equipment, etc.

- Display fresh or silk flowers.

STEP NINE: BLESSINGS

This last step is optional — it's for those of you who wish to bring your sense of spirituality into using Feng Shui.

In BTB Feng Shui, it is believed that the physical moving of objects is only one part of achieving the desired Feng Shui results. To get the full benefit, changes must be started with intention and should be finished with a blessing. Blessings can be done using prayer, meditation or visualization. You can create your own blessings based on your personal spiritual beliefs and prayers — or you can try the Three Secrets Reinforcement, a traditional BTB Feng Shui blessing. I have also included the Orange Lotus Blessing.

Three Secrets Reinforcement

The Three Secrets Reinforcement uses body, speech and mind to enhance Feng Shui techniques and improve your environmental and personal Chi.

Body — hand gesture (mudra) to express the power of the body

Speech — mantra or prayer

Mind — visualization of the intended result

The Three Secrets Reinforcement mudra is a gesture with the hands to remove obstacles and to reinforce your goals. The mudra is used to remove negativity. Usually, women use their left hand while men use their right hand. The two middle fingers are bent and the thumb is placed on top of their fingernails. The index finger and baby finger are extended. Flick the middle fingers outwards nine times. Imagine light coming out of your fingers getting rid of the bad Chi and boosting the positive Chi.

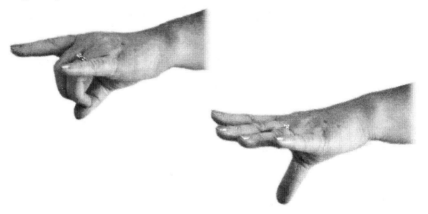

The secret mantra is *om mani pad me hum*, which attracts the power of compassion and accomplishment. Any other personal prayer or blessing is appropriate, for example, *Our Father*.

The mind secret involves visualizing the intended result — what you want to happen. Remember to visualize this result happening step-by-step, including a beginning, middle and end. Invoke the five senses to make it real.

Repeat the mudra, mantra and mind reinforcement nine times.

Orange Lotus Blessing

The Orange Lotus Blessing, another effective blessing, can be done using an orange cut to symbolize a lotus flower. Wash an orange and cut it (not all the way through) so that it has nine petals. Remove the flesh, so that you are left with only the peel.

Place the orange peel in a bowl with some cooled boiled water. Bless your home using *om mani pad me hum* (or an appropriate prayer of your own) and flicking the water using the hand mudra described. Flick nine times in each zone.

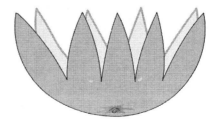

Now you have completed the Nine Steps to the Feng Shui Zone and I hope you've kept a note in your journal of all the changes you've made. You're probably up to number 50 by now! The key here is to pay attention to the changes in your life. Feng Shui will get you to your goals; it just may not take the route you expected. I worked with a client with huge financial difficulties. She implemented changes throughout her home, with special attention paid to the Prosperity zone. Two months later she was forced into bankruptcy. You may think that was a terrible outcome of Feng Shui, but a year later she was debt free, she didn't lose her house or her business, and her business is now flourishing. The Universe will give you everything you need, you just have to ask.

Applying the Nine Steps

5

Applying the Nine Steps

Now that you have been introduced to the Nine Steps — including step eight, cures for specific zones — I will show you how to apply cures to specific environments. I give examples for your home, your lot, your garden and your neighbourhood. I also suggest cures for your apartment, office and desk and car, and I have added cures for special circumstances — college rooms and hospitals. I close this section with stories of specific cures I have used in difficult situations.

Before applying the cures to these environments, remember to use the Nine Steps:

Step One: Setting Intentions

Step Two: Starting the Chi Flowing

Step Three: Clearing Outer Clutter

Step Four: Clearing Inner Clutter

Step Five: Personal Care

Step Six: Setting Personal Goals

Step Seven: Choosing Improvement

Step Eight: Applying Cures to Zones

Step Nine: Blessings

YOUR HOME — INSIDE

How your house is laid out will affect both your environmental Chi and your personal Chi. Is the Chi flowing freely in each room and through-out your home? Is the Chi dead or robust? Your floor plan will make a difference. For those of you who are planning to build a new home, I suggest the best placement for the rooms. I also discuss how to over-come some of the difficulties caused by your house layout.

Planning to Build Your Home

There are rooms in your home that benefit from the active or Yang Chi at the front of the home, and there are rooms that benefit from the more Yin or passive Chi at the back of the home. Rooms that benefit from being at the front of your home are the foyer, living room, family room, study, office, guest bedroom and older-child bedroom. Good rooms at the back of your home are the kitchen, master bedroom, dining room and bathroom. The living room, family room and study work well in the centre of the home too. Avoid placing the kitchen or bathroom in the centre of the home because you do not want to see these rooms from the front door; do not place a staircase or fireplace in the centre of the home because you will create rushing, argumentative Chi.

For you new home builders out there, the ideal position of each room, according to the Bagua map, is:

Master bedroom	Prosperity, Fame or Relationship and Love zones
Living room	Health zone
Study/Home office	Career and Life Path or Skills and Knowledge zones
Family room	Family zone

Dining room	Prosperity, Fame or Relationship and Love zones
Child's bedroom	Creativity and Children zone
Kitchen	Family, Prosperity, Fame or Creativity and Children zones
Guest or older-child bedroom	Helpful People and Travel zone

Opposite is one suggestion for a single-storey house layout.

The first impression that anyone gets of your home sets the tone for their whole experience. It also affects you. The first room that you enter every time you come home affects your psychology and health. Energy follows attention. What I mean by this is, wherever your attention goes, energy follows. If a pile of clutter takes your attention when you enter your home, the energy that is entering your home is going there too and your personal energy will follow. An uplifting and beautiful entrance to your home will increase the energy flow to the entire house and give you a personal energy boost at the same time.

Energy follows attention, money follows energy, health follows energy.

HOUSE PLAN ZONES AND ROOM

PROSPERITY ZONE Kitchen	FAME ZONE Dining Room	RELATIONSHIPS AND LOVE ZONE Master Bedroom
		Bathroom
FAMILY ZONE Family Room	HEALTH ZONE Living Room	Bathroom
		CREATIVITY AND CHILDREN ZONE Child's Bedroom
SKILLS AND KNOWLEDGE ZONE Study	CAREER AND LIFEPATH ZONE Entrance Hall	HELPFUL PEOPLE AND TRAVEL ZONE Teenage Bedroom

Front Door

Cures for Your House Layout

Perhaps you realize that your house layout is not the most beneficial for the Chi to flow. Don't worry! There really is a cure for every Feng Shui problem. In China, it was always thought that if you called in a Feng Shui Practitioner to assist you with your energy problems, you might as well start packing before she even saw your home, as the advice was usually that you had to move. I believe that there is a Feng Shui solution for every energy problem, every home can be cured. Following are some solutions for you to try.

Missing Pieces

The ideal shapes in Feng Shui are the circle, oval, square and rectangle — all solid regular shapes. When you lay the Bagua map over your home's footprint, notice whether you have any missing pieces or incomplete areas. For instance, when the back left corner of your home is missing, you might have trouble hanging onto your money (your Prosperity zone is missing). Similarly, if the back central zone is missing, you might be having problems with your reputation in town (your Fame zone is missing).

MISSING PIECES

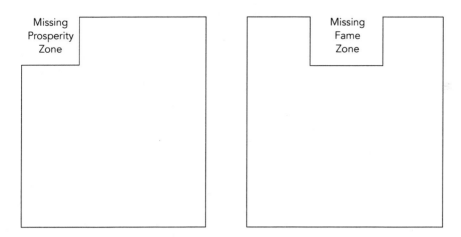

Missing Prosperity Zone

Missing Fame Zone

Cures for Missing Pieces

On the inside of the house facing the missing piece, hang a crystal, position a healthy rounded-leaf plant (or silk plant) or hang a mirror. On the outside of the house in the missing piece, place a Bagua mirror (see below for description of a Bagua mirror) or a bright light. Plant a good-sized bush or tree exactly at the place where the two walls would meet if the piece were not missing. Or you could bury red string along the lines where the walls would be, to complete the missing piece. You could also paint a red line or place three or nine boulders at the point where the two lines should meet.

MISSING PIECES CURES

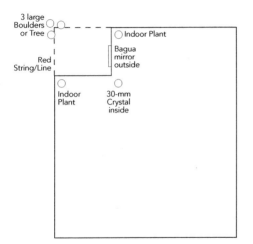

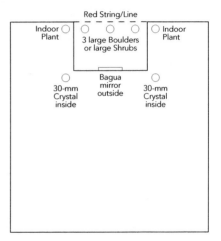

More Simple Cures

- As stated previously, the entranceway is very important. If you can see the stove (which should ideally be placed in a kitchen at the back of your home), the toilet or the bed from the entranceway, your personal Chi will be impacted negatively. The person cooking at the stove will feel vulnerable (hang a crystal above their head to settle them down) and be aware that there will be a focus on food, which could cause weight problems. If the first thing you see is the toilet . . . need I say more? Always keep the door closed to the room with the toilet and deflect the Chi by hanging a mirror on the outside of the door. The bed protects you and provides rest; you could feel vulnerable if your bed has no privacy from the front door. Keep the bedroom door closed all the time.

- An interior stairway facing the front door signifies money rolling out of the house. Gravity pushes the Chi of the house down the stairs and out the door. The cure for this is to hang a 30-mm (1") crystal or wind chime halfway between the front door and the base of the stairs. (Remember to hang it using nine inches of red string.)

- If you can see from the front door to the back door, your Chi is coming in the front door and rushing out the back door and this will make it hard for you to hold onto your money. As a cure, place a large (40-mm or 1 ½") crystal or wind chime midway along the corridor to disperse the rushing Chi.

- Beams over a bed or above a desk have a negative impact. The cure for this is to paint the beam the same colour as the ceiling and place two bamboo flutes at 45 degree angles (with the mouthpiece down) along the beam.

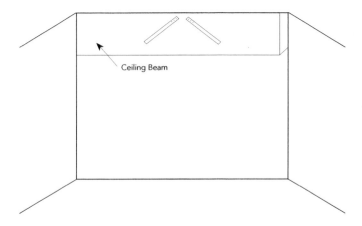

Ceiling Beam

- Pillars can block Chi. The cure for a pillar is to mirror it on all four sides or to cover it with silk ivy to transform it into a tree.

- Skylights that are put in when the house is being built pose no problems. Adding a skylight into the roof after a house is built is like cutting into your back. Hang 30-mm (1") crystals in all skylights to cure this.

- Empty doors, created by a doorframe with no physical door, can cause a husband or wife to leave home. Replace the door or hang a beaded or regular curtain there to replace the door.

- "Arguing doors" exist in a home where the doors opposite each other (e.g., down a passageway) overlap and are not exactly aligned opposite each other. As you can imagine, Arguing Doors cause chaotic Chi and are the cause of dissension for the residents of the home. In a home that I recently viewed, on the second floor there were four doors clustered around a small landing. All of them were arguing — the master bedroom door with the study door and the second bedroom door with the bathroom door. This was also the place where the family arguments usually began. A quick and easy cure for this is to place square or rectangular mirrors at eye level beside each door.

This is the wonderful thing about BTB Feng Shui: there is a solution for every problem (opportunity?). Although I must confess, I am looking forward to the day when I am able to build my own perfectly, perfect Feng Shui home!

YOUR HOME — OUTSIDE

All of our work so far has been on the inside of your home, but the exterior of your house and property (lot) is equally as important. A basic truth of Feng Shui is that everything you see coming and going to and from your home affects your energy. Be aware of the fact that the energy around you is ever changing. The energy of your neighbourhood is affected by weather, buildings (and the Chi within those buildings), construction, roads and much more. This energy is fluid —like wind and water — and your task is to attract enough good Chi into your home. Imagine a gentle breeze or babbling stream. As the Chi on the exterior is changing, so the Chi on the interior is being affected. Nothing stays the same. Make adjustments to your interior environment as you feel changes happening to parts of your life.

One of the cures I suggest using for outside your home is the Bagua mirror. The correct Bagua mirror is made of wood, it is eight-sided with a circular mirror in the middle, coloured red and green, and has the Chinese trigrams printed on it. Bagua mirrors should *only* be hung facing the outside of your home, they should NEVER be facing into your living space. Information on how to find these mirrors is in the

Resources section. Don't be tempted to put up fancier-looking Bagua mirrors; none of them is as effective as a plain wooden one.

Bagua Mirror

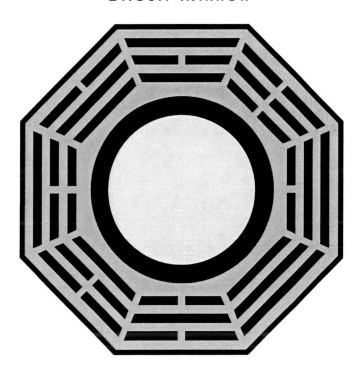

Reading the Chi in Your Neighbourhood

Take an objective look at your neighbourhood. Are the pets well cared for, the wildlife and birds abundant and healthy? Are the plants and trees healthy, growing and flourishing? If the answer is yes, then you can rest assured that the Chi of your neighbourhood is healthy. If the answer is no or somewhat, then work needs to be done to improve the energy around your home. A quick cure is to add moving water to the front yard, but read on and I'll show you more solutions.

Another important observation when reading the Chi of your neighbourhood is to notice what is going on in the lives of your neighbours. Are they cheerful and friendly? If you have difficult neighbours, plant a hedge along that boundary, hang a wind chime or place a Bagua mirror on the wall facing their house. If you have problem neighbours in your apartment building, you can hang the Bagua mirror facing them on an adjoining wall; the Bagua mirror will deflect unwanted negative energy. (Remember to *never* hang a Bagua mirror facing into your living space.)

What recent life occurrences have there been in your neighbourhood

— births, deaths, job losses, divorces and accidents? A client of mine had an unusual set of things happen in her neighbourhood — huge life-changing occurrences happened to the neighbours on both sides of her. On one side, the breadwinner in the home suddenly lost his job and on the other side, one of the occupants died suddenly. Both life experiences caused negative Chi, not only to the neighbours but also to my client. A quick cure was to place Bagua mirrors (or she could have used wind chimes) on the outside of her house facing each neighbour. This deflected the negative Chi, provided protection and ensured that the good Chi stayed in her home.

If you have an Institution next door, opposite or behind your home, beware of negative energy. Institutions include cemeteries or funeral homes (full of dead Chi), hospitals or long-term care facilities, police or fire stations, schools or churches. A cure for an Institution that is too nearby is to hang a Bagua mirror on or near the outside of the front door or to hang the Bagua mirror so that it is facing the Institution.

In some modern neighbourhoods the houses are built very close together. If this is the case for your home, hang a Bagua mirror facing the other houses or buildings. If your home is too close to a highway, train tracks or airport, plant a tall hedge or have flagpoles with colourful flags along that side of your property.

Roads and Streets

Activity Level: The street you live on is the main source of energy for your home and life. Brisk, lively energy is best — not too active, not too quiet. Too little energy brings low Chi into your home, which is bad for finances and health; while too much rushing Chi brings chaos and disruption into your life.

- If you live on a very busy street, which causes rushing energy, you could plant a hedge or build a fence to slow the Chi down. Hang a wind chime at the front door and place a Bagua mirror on or near the outside of the front door.

- If you live on a street that is too quiet and therefore has stagnant energy, you should introduce moving water to the front of your lot, erect flags, make sure that you have bright outdoor lights and add bird feeders to the garden.

The shape of the road and how it moves past your home is important too.

- If you are lucky enough to have a road that curves towards your home you will have good finances, successful children and goals achieved.

- If the road curves away from your house, you will find it easy to lose money and to not take advantage of opportunities. To cure this, place a Bagua mirror on or near the outside of the front door.

- If your home is at the end of a T-junction the strength of the flow of Chi will harm your health, finances and relationships. Once again, the cure for this is to hang a Bagua mirror on or near the outside of the front door.

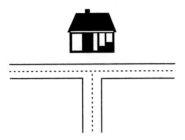

- If you have roads on either side of your house, there will be pressure in your family life and career. Plant a hedge or install three flagpoles on both sides of your house.

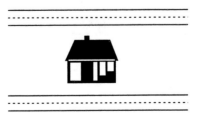

◑ If you live on a cul-de-sac, the Chi is draining out of all the homes. Ideally you should place a traffic circle with trees in the centre of the cul-de-sac. If this is not possible, protect your own home with tall trees, a Bagua mirror placed near the front door and moving water in the front yard.

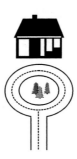

Property/Lot

The best position for your house on the lot is the "armchair" or command position. The best position for your house is to be situated in the middle of the lot front to back and left to right, with the road below and the lot rising up slightly behind. Trees or houses on either side provide the armrests. The front ⅓ of your lot represents your past, the middle ⅓ your present and the back ⅓ your future. The front ⅓ is where opportunities begin, the middle ⅓ is where situations develop and the back ⅓ is where your wealth is stored. The front ⅓ represents planting, the middle ⅓ growing and the back ⅓ harvesting.

- Land that slopes away behind the house represents negative Chi and decreased wealth and money. The cure for this is to mount a light on a tree or pole behind the house to shine on the roof of your house. This is a very strong method to lift the Chi of the home.

- If your house is below the road, place a bright light behind the house shining up towards the road, line the sides of the driveway with lights or use three flagpoles with colourful flags.

- Lighting on the outside of your home is very important. Balance your home by having a spotlight above the front door or have bright lights on either side of the front door to act like guardians. Motion-sensor lights that turn on automatically as you enter an area encourage clear thinking and create a feeling of space and flowing Chi.

Garden

We all know that a beautiful garden lifts our spirits. Plants share their energy with us and healthy thriving Chi is all around in a well-cared-for garden. There is a lot you can do in your garden using Feng Shui techniques. I am including only a few suggestions.

- If you add trees to your garden you will add vitality, growth and new life and you will increase the living Chi. There are some trees that are better than others and umbrella-shaped trees are particularity good at providing protection and safety. Evergreen trees are better than deciduous ones and trees that have flowers and fruit have wonderful Chi. Avoid weeping willows which have down Chi. Also avoid trees with thorns. Remember, do not plant a tree directly in front of your front door and don't have trees that are dying or unhealthy in your yard.

- Lay the Bagua map over your yard, placing the Career and Life Path zone at the road. You can lay the Bagua map over the front yard and the back yard separately, or over the entire lot in one go.

GARDEN BAGUA MAP PLACEMENT #1
Lay Bagua Map over entire lot (preferred)

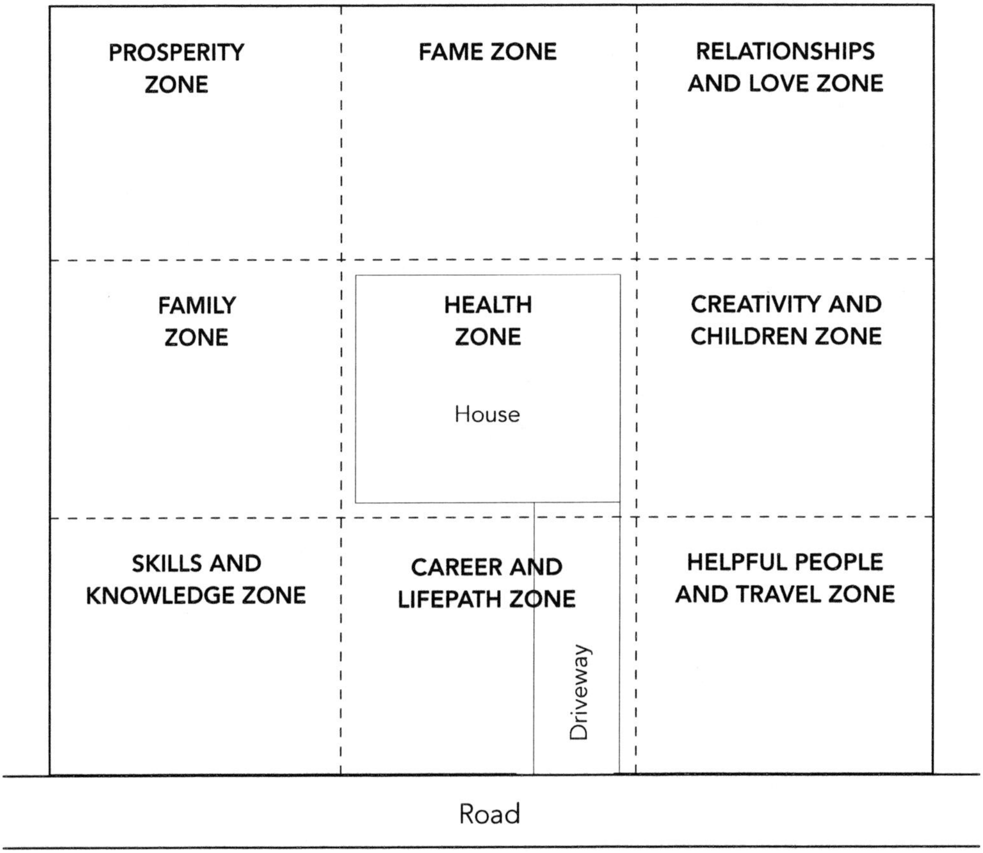

PROSPERITY ZONE	FAME ZONE	RELATIONSHIPS AND LOVE ZONE
FAMILY ZONE	HEALTH ZONE House	CREATIVITY AND CHILDREN ZONE
SKILLS AND KNOWLEDGE ZONE	CAREER AND LIFEPATH ZONE	HELPFUL PEOPLE AND TRAVEL ZONE

Driveway

Road

GARDEN BAGUA MAP PLACEMENT #2

Lay Bagua Map over front and back yards separately

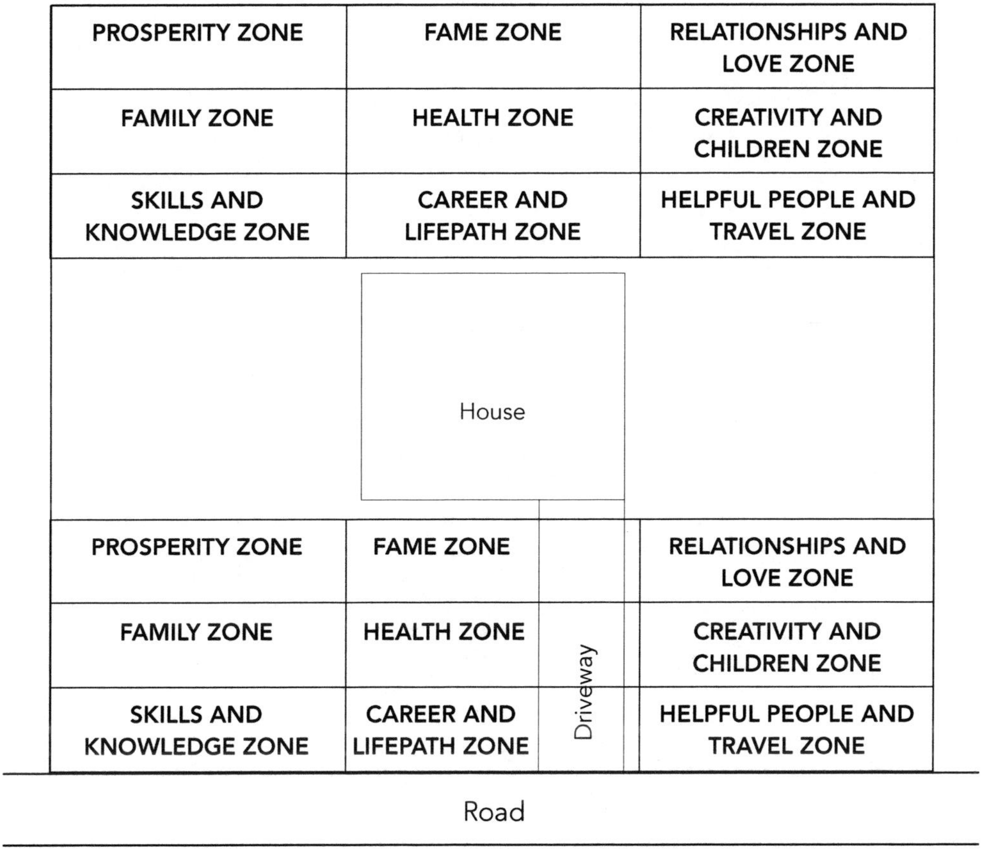

PROSPERITY ZONE	FAME ZONE	RELATIONSHIPS AND LOVE ZONE
FAMILY ZONE	HEALTH ZONE	CREATIVITY AND CHILDREN ZONE
SKILLS AND KNOWLEDGE ZONE	CAREER AND LIFEPATH ZONE	HELPFUL PEOPLE AND TRAVEL ZONE

House

PROSPERITY ZONE	FAME ZONE		RELATIONSHIPS AND LOVE ZONE
FAMILY ZONE	HEALTH ZONE		CREATIVITY AND CHILDREN ZONE
SKILLS AND KNOWLEDGE ZONE	CAREER AND LIFEPATH ZONE	Driveway	HELPFUL PEOPLE AND TRAVEL ZONE

Road

- Plant a four-seasons Feng Shui garden using the colours of the Bagua map and choose vigorous plants with lots of colour. It is better to purchase a few healthy, thriving plants from a reputable garden centre than to fill your garden with less expensive weak ones that will have weak and unhealthy Chi. At my suggestion, a young couple getting ready to have a family planted a pink flowering cherry tree in their Relationship and Love zone and let nature do the rest!

- Add moving water to the front of your yard to improve cash and finances. Actually I can't think of any reason not to have moving water in the front yard. At one client's front door we simply filled a large ceramic pot with water, inserted a small pump fountain (purchased at the local garden centre) and voila — a gorgeous water feature for little cost!

- Hang a wind chime at the front door to attract Chi. Clear away any vegetation cluttering up the front door. This is very important. If you can move freely and easily to and from the "Mouth of Chi", so can the energy. Trim back branches, bushes and hedges that are blocking the front door and front path.

House Numbers

House numbers should always be mounted in a straight horizontal line, not vertically or at an angle. The number of your house influences your home's unique personality and makes it different from the home next door. To find out what this number means, add your house numbers together until you have one number. For example 2790 Elm Street becomes 2+7+9+0 = 18 and 1+8 = 9. If you live in an apartment, you need to add the unit number to the street number. For example Apt 102, 3456 Oak Street becomes 1+0+2+3+4+5+6 = 21 and 2+1 = 3. If your street is numbered, for example 29th Street, do not include this in the count as the street number or name affects the entire street, not just your home.

1   is a house of independence and individuality.
2   is a house of partnership and relationships.
3   is a house of communication and fun.
4   is a house of hard work and organization.
5   is a house of adventure and travel.
6   is a house for family that is warm and welcoming.
7   is a quiet, solitary house for a spiritual journey.
8   is a house of success and material prosperity.
9   is a house of service — a Mother Theresa house.

If you are interested in learning more about Numerology, I recommend *The Everything Numerology Book* by Ellae Elinwood.

There is a cure for everything in Feng Shui, so don't feel that you need to move out of your home because you are concerned about the house number. Simply be aware of the nature of the home and act accordingly. If you live in a number-4 home (which represents work, work, work), then schedule time for family members to have some fun.

YOUR APARTMENT

There are some particular challenges for those of you who live in apartments. Even if you are renting, always treat the place as your own home. Create an environment that will support and enhance your personal Chi. Get the apartment into the Feng Shui Zone to ensure that you create energy that will have a positive impact on your life success.

Whether you live in a high-rise building or not, you need to ground yourself in the building (because of the close proximity of your neighbours). Place smooth, rounded rocks and healthy plants in the four outermost corners of your apartment. Add large mirrors and crystals to the apartment to create a feeling of more space and expand the Chi. Mirrors also expand out the walls of your apartment, creating harmony with your neighbours.

Remember, if you have difficult neighbours, you should hang a Bagua mirror facing them on an adjoining wall. The Bagua mirror will deflect unwanted negative energy and keep the positive energy in your home. (Never hang a Bagua mirror facing into your living space.)

YOUR OFFICE AND DESK

I am often asked whether Feng Shui works at the office. If getting the energy moving in your home is important, then so is getting the energy moving in your office. As you know, you can place the Bagua map on a room, but getting down to a more micro level, you can also place the Bagua map on your desk itself. Here are some suggestions for rearranging your office and desk. Remember, you can use any of the energy adjustments referred to on the Bagua map, provided they are in the correct zone. These cures will improve, change and add positive energy.

Your Office Space

Use the Bagua map to show you where each zone is in your office space, by placing the Career and Life Path zone in the centre of the wall containing the door to your office. Here are some suggestions to enhance the Chi in each zone:

- Place water in the Career Zone — this could be a small water feature, a picture of water or a mirror.

- Your books should go in the Skills and Knowledge Zone — don't forget to only keep books that inspire you.

- A silk or real plant should go into the Family Zone.

- Place something of value in the Prosperity Zone.

- Your awards and qualifications belong in your Fame Zone.

- Put a photo of your significant other in the Relationship Zone.

- Photos of your children go into the Creativity and Children Zone

- Your Rolodex belongs in the Helpful People Zone.

- Place your computer in the Prosperity Zone if possible. If that doesn't work, the computer could go into either of the metal zones, which are Creativity and Children or Helpful People and Travel.

Remember that these cures can be applied to the whole room or to the desk space only. Try to include the correct colour for each Bagua zone in the room. One appropriate cure per zone, with the correct colour, is sufficient.

Your Desk

Some further ways to boost the energy at work are to:

- Tape a coloured and laminated Bagua map under your desk with

DESK BAGUA MAP PLACEMENT

PROSPERITY ZONE	FAME ZONE	RELATIONSHIPS AND LOVE ZONE
FAMILY ZONE	HEALTH ZONE	CREATIVITY AND CHILDREN ZONE
SKILLS AND KNOWLEDGE ZONE	CAREER AND LIFEPATH ZONE	HELPFUL PEOPLE AND TRAVEL ZONE

Chair

the Fame Zone farthest away from you and the Bagua map facing up. The reason we do this is that the Bagua map will enhance and balance the energy around your desk.

- Position your desk so that you can see the door to the office — never sit with your back to the door. The "command position" is especially important in your office. I see more problems in offices with people who sit with their backs to the door than anything else. If this is unavoidable, place a small mirror to reflect behind you.

- Hang a crystal (30-mm or 1") from the ceiling directly over the position of your head when sitting at your desk, to promote clarity of thought.

- Place red on the back of your office chair for strength — anything will do, a piece of red tape, red sweater, etc.

- If your business/job relies on the telephone, tie nine red ribbons (nine inches in length each) around the phone line. Red is the colour of power in Feng Shui and nine is the number of completion. These ribbons will add power to your telephone business dealings.

All of these suggestions for your office and desk, apply to your home office too.

YOUR CAR

I once had a client whose office was a study in clutter. There were papers, boxes and stuff everywhere. During our discussions about his Feng Shui needs he happened to mention that his car was always spotless. This was also the place where he got all his best thinking done. Imagine that!

- Keep the outside of your car clean — make a promise to wash it once a week.

- Clean the inside once a week too — dust and vacuum. Add

essential oils to the interior for fragrance; try to avoid synthetic car fresheners.

- Hang a 20-mm (¾") crystal in the car for protection and clarity of thought. I hang mine from my rearview mirror, but out of my line of sight.

- Place a coloured and laminated Bagua map under the driver's seat with the Fame Zone pointing towards the engine, face up, and this will balance the energy in your vehicle.

There are few things better than getting into a car that is clean and smells good. It is a wonderful way to start a trip and helps you have a positive frame of mind every day.

COLLEGE ROOM

Both of our sons left home to attend school 3,000 kms away. It was a great reassurance to me to be able to give them the protection of

Feng Shui and I thought I would share my plan for a College bedroom with you. This plan actually works for any bedroom, but I designed it for my boys' bedroom in their home away from home.

- Laminate two coloured Bagua maps and place one under the mattress (Fame zone facing the head and facing upwards) and one under the desk (Fame zone facing away from the chair and facing upwards).

- In the Prosperity zone: a silk plant, mirror or picture of something prosperous.

- In the Fame zone: a poster of a famous person, red flag or their certificates and achievements.

- In the Relationships and Love zone: pictures of friends and good times.

- In the Creativity and Children zone: computer, desk lamp, fridge, or perhaps a favourite stuffed animal.

COLLEGE ROOM CURES

PROSPERITY ZONE	FAME ZONE	RELATIONSHIPS AND LOVE ZONE
Silk plant Mirror	Poster of famous people Red flag Certificates and Achievements	Pictures of friends and good times
FAMILY ZONE	**HEALTH ZONE**	**CREATIVITY AND CHILDREN ZONE**
Photos of family	Yellow/Earth tone rug	Computer Desk lamp Fridge Stuffed animal
SKILLS AND KNOWLEDGE ZONE	**CAREER AND LIFEPATH ZONE**	**HELPFUL PEOPLE AND TRAVEL ZONE**
Round, heavy rocks Books	Mirror Black rug Picture of water	Mirror Spiritual item

- In the Helpful People and Travel zone: a round mirror or a photo or statue of a helpful person (e.g., favourite grandparent, angel, Buddha, etc.).

- In the Career and Life Path zone: a mirror, black rug or picture of water.

- In the Skills and Knowledge zone: smooth, round heavy rocks and books.

- In the Family zone: photos of the family.

- In the Health zone: a yellow or earth-toned rug.

- Try to include the appropriate colour for each Bagua zone in the room in their correct position.

- And finally, place something red on the bed — pillow, throw, stuffed animal — to boost their personal Chi.

It isn't easy having children leave home, but I certainly found it easier being confident in the knowledge that the Chi of their surroundings was working for them rather than against them. What a powerful friend!

HOSPITAL ROOM AND BED

Several people have asked me whether Feng Shui can be used in a hospital room. The Feng Shui challenge here is twofold: how to block out all the negative energy from the other sick patients; and how to improve health through enhancing the health zone.

Here are some simple cures:

- To block out and disperse sick energy: hang a crystal from the bed, preferably near the head of the patient. This crystal should be round and at least 30-mm (1") in diameter and should be hung using a nine-inch red ribbon.

- To absorb and deflect the negative Chi of the institution: surround the patient with nine healthy plants. These plants should have rounded leaves — purple flowering African violets are very beneficial. They'll do a great job in the Prosperity zone when the patient gets home too!

- To lift the personal Chi of the patient: place fresh flowers, aromatherapy oils and candles around them, and for an added boost, place a red throw or cushion on the bed. (It is not essential to light the candles, they carry the energy of fire whether they are lit or not.)

- Introduce lots of yellow — yellow towels, bathrobe, washcloths and nightgown — to boost their health zone.

- Don't forget to include this person in your prayers, visualizations (with a successful outcome) and meditations.

FENG SHUI SUCCESS STORIES

As you move through your own home implementing Feng Shui cures, there will be times when you won't know what to do. Stand still and listen to the Chi, trust your intuition. Below are some of the more inter-esting practical situations that I have found.

Grey House

I was invited to visit a home that was situated on the waterfront in a city. This home was gorgeous and well loved. The couple who lived there had bought the lot, dreamed about the home, planned it and built it together. It was their "baby," their retirement dream.

Yet, something was out of balance and they couldn't quite put their finger on it. I isolated two main issues. The front door had a large glass panel — almost the size of the entire door. This symbolized a lack of security and strength for the home, they were vulnerable. I suggested that the door be replaced with a solid one.

The other imbalance was that the entire main floor was in shades of grey, with very few other colours. The walls were grey, the furniture was grey, the appliances were steel, and on and on. Grey is a colour that can mean harmony or frustration, and in this case the colour was having a negative effect because it was too overpowering, too much of one thing. I suggested balancing the home by adding the colour red. Red is the colour of fire (grey is the colour of metal and fire melts metal). The client added red to each room with accents. We also added nine healthy plants to the main floor to lift the Chi — 9 is the number of completion in Feng Shui.

Sick Apartment

Without a doubt this home was my biggest challenge. The client had lived in this apartment for three years. Her health was deteriorating, her neighbours were moving in and out (she'd had eight neighbours since she had moved in) and below her bedroom was the consulting office for a family physician. This home literally smelled sick, and the sick Chi coming up from the doctor's office was overpowering her.

After making sure that her front door, stove and bedroom were in the Feng Shui Zone, we placed a Bagua mirror under her bed, facing down towards the doctor's rooms; we hung a Bagua mirror above her front door; she practiced EFT everyday (refer to the Resources section) and she adjusted her personal Chi with bath cures and meditation.

Quiet Street in a Seniors' Complex

A recently-retired couple had built a home in a secure and beautiful seniors' complex. The complex was quiet, the street was even quieter and their front door was tucked away to the side of the house. Getting Chi into the home was the big challenge.

We decided to place a large boulder at the end of the driveway — near the street — with the house number on it. The boulder provided stability and strength for the home and attracted Chi onto the lot. A large tree planted near the street (we picked a flowering cherry) attracted attention and energy, and a flagpole was erected near the front door.

Vulnerable Bed

I must say that it was of grave concern to me to see a client's bed not only in the death position (feet facing directly out of the door), but also placed right underneath a huge bedroom window (no stability or strength for the bed at all). The bed had to move — immediately — but the only other place for it was facing a large wall mirror. We decided to move the bed into that position, but to cure the effects of the mirror by hanging a 40-mm (1 ½") crystal halfway between the foot of the bed and the mirror. We also hung a curtain in front of the mirror, which could be drawn closed when they were sleeping.

Acreage

Living out in the country can be a wonderful experience, but it also can come with some very particular energy problems. This house was set back from the road and had a very long driveway. There was no identifying sign for the home at the road, the turn-off to the driveway was difficult to find and impossible in the dark. The Chi had the same difficulty finding the house as the visitors did.

The home needed two bright lights at the end of the driveway along with a clear and easy-to-see identifying sign (house or lot number); lights lining the driveway showing the way clearly to the front door; a bright light and a large wind chime at the front door.

True Love

The Feng Shui successes are too many to list, but this is one of my favourites. I have a dear friend in another city that I visit about three times a year. She'd been divorced for four years and was starting to feel ready for a new relationship. I gave her a small heart-shaped container (representing the energy of romance and love) with a slip of paper inside that read, "I will find the one!" (a clear affirmation for what she hoped to achieve). I instructed her to put the container in the Relationship and Love zone of her bedroom and perform the Three Secrets Visualization (Step Nine). About a month later, she called to say that she had found him. She had fallen in love with the man who had been a great friend and support to her over those four difficult years since the divorce.

Here's a very important reality for those of you who are setting up a home with a new partner: only bring things into the relationship that you love or need. Leave room for "together" things. Don't crowd your new home and new relationship with things that remind you of a previous life. (I hope I don't have to stress the need for a new bed.)

Expect the Unexpected

Doing this work on your home, bringing it into the Feng Shui Zone, will cause positive change in your life. This change doesn't always follow an expected route. A woman participated in one of my workshops. Her most pressing need was to find a way to fix her relationship with her daughter-in-law. Nothing was going well between them. We adjusted the energy in her home and she was really looking forward to their next visit. To her shock, they had a huge blow-up, which resulted in a king-sized fight. My student was confused and thought Feng Shui wasn't working — not in the way she expected anyway. But the result of this fight was that they ended up in counselling together. Needless to say the relationship is on a sound footing now. Feng Shui will get you to your goal; it just may not follow the path you thought it would!

6

Resource Section

- The I Ching — Yin and Yang
- Emotional Freedom Technique
- Visualizations
- Colour in Your Home
- Five Element Chart
- Bagua Map
- Annotated Bibliography
- Internet Resources
- Feng Shui Items Available
- Making Contact

6

Resource Section

In this section I offer a number of resources. These include brief introductions to the I Ching and EFT (Emotional Freedom Technique) — additional and complementary tools to Feng Shui. I also include some easy-to-follow visualizations, a colour reference section, the Five Element Chart and Bagua map for quick reference, a bibliography, internet resources list, and information on how to contact me for workshops, book and supply purchases.

THE I CHING — YIN AND YANG

Let's take a little sojourn into another wonderful Chinese teaching

—the I Ching. The I Ching is an ancient teaching that can be used to give you guidance when you need to make important decisions in your life. I will give a very brief introduction to I Ching. There are many I Ching books available in bookstores; my favourite is *Teach Yourself I Ching* by Andy Baggott.

History

The roots of the I Ching go back thousands of years to a time when the sages of ancient China began to try to find ways of understanding the Universe. They wanted to understand the underlying patterns that existed in the Universe, so that they could begin to predict how those patterns might evolve and thus, be able to predict the future. This sounds very similar to Feng Shui, doesn't it? If we balance the energy of our surroundings, we affect our personal Chi and therefore have a positive impact on all areas of our life, including our future life success.

The ancient Chinese believed that the Universe was composed of two opposite and complementary forces or energies — Yin and Yang. Yin and Yang exist together and describe the primary qualities of all existing things. Nothing is fully Yin or fully Yang — all things contain energy from both. In your home, Feng Shui seeks to bring about a balance of Yin and Yang energy, creating a harmonious environment that will bring good health, abundance and peace.

Yin Yang Symbol

From the forces of Yin and Yang, eight trigrams (pa kua) were developed Trigrams were developed from Yin and Yang and linked to nature: Heaven and Earth, Fire and Water, Thunder and Wind, Mountain and Lake.

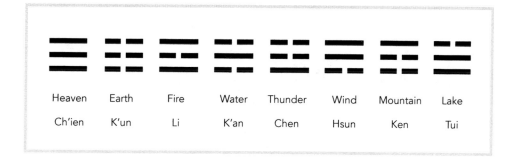

Heaven	Earth	Fire	Water	Thunder	Wind	Mountain	Lake
Ch'ien	K'un	Li	K'an	Chen	Hsun	Ken	Tui

The I Ching describes nature and the workings of the Universe through symbols and images. Each trigram has a symbol and an ancient meaning. Two trigrams are combined to form a hexagram. When two trigrams are joined to form a hexagram, a new image is formed with a new symbolism. The core meanings of these hexagrams form the basis of I Ching.

How to Use the I Ching

To do an I Ching reading you need a pen and paper, three (washed) coins of the same size and denomination, a question to be asked and *The Book of Changes* to help interpret the I Ching. You can ask any question, from "Should I buy this house?" to "Where am I in my life?" Repeat the question and throw the coins, then follow the instructions in Chapter 5 of *Teach Yourself I Ching*.

Understanding the I Ching

Over thousands of years, people using the I Ching have testified to its accuracy. How can it be so accurate? Carl Jung, the Swiss doctor known for his explorations into the human psyche and for coining the term "the collective unconscious," used the I Ching. He believed that the subconscious had a great deal to do with the weird accuracy of the I Ching. How? When we consult the I Ching for a reading, our subconscious mind affects the outcome because it already knows the answer.

> *Consulting the Book of Changes at a time of personal crisis amounts almost to a session with your favourite psychoanalyst. There is nothing in the fall of the coins or in the text of the book that is not already in you; all the I Ching does, with its beautifully organized patterns, is to draw the necessary information and decisions out and to absolve the conscious mind of the burden of responsibility for these decisions.*
>
> Colin Wilson, quoted in *Supernature*, Lyall Watson, pp. 301–2

My husband and I have used the I Ching with absolute confidence when we've needed to make big decisions. I also do I Ching readings in my workshops, either individually or for groups. With practice, it is possible to learn how to do a reading for yourself. Respect the I Ching — it is not a party trick, and it will assist you at those important times in your life. Be grateful for the thousands of years of wisdom and power that come with an I Ching reading.

EMOTIONAL FREEDOM TECHNIQUE

I learned of the Emotional Freedom Technique just a few years ago and by my own definition, the Emotional Freedom Technique is a combination of "do-it-yourself" (DIY) acupressure and visualization. By this I mean that tapping the body in key places will release a flow of energy to improve mental and physical health. Improved energy flow means improved healing — both of body and mind.

EFT is based on the fact that "the cause of *all* negative emotions is a disruption in the body's energy system." EFT is a way to clear and heal this disruption, allowing personal Chi to flow smoothly.

Full details on this incredible technique and the documented results they are achieving are on the EFT website, www.emofree.com

Based on impressive new discoveries involving the

body's subtle energies, EFT has been clinically effective in thousands of cases for Trauma & Abuse, Stress & Anxiety, Fears & Phobias, Depression, Addictive Cravings, Children's Issues and hundreds of physical symptoms including headaches, body pains and breathing difficulties. Properly applied, over 80% achieve either noticeable improvement or complete cessation of the problem. It is the missing piece to the healing puzzle.

Emotional Freedom Technique, www.emofree.com, Gary Craig, CA

Use this DIY acupressure and visualization on any emotional or physical problem and be persistent until the problem disappears. EFT can be used as often as you need it during the day. The success stories are too many to list, but I will share one with you. My client's husband was a chronic insomniac and nothing seemed to help him get a good night's sleep. His work was suffering and there was considerable strain on their marriage. First we applied the principles of Feng Shui to his bedroom, and then I taught him EFT. It has worked wonders. He does not always sleep right through the night, but when he does waken, he simply does his EFT tapping routine and falls straight back to sleep. Persevere with any physical or emotional problem and it will help you enormously.

On the EFT website go to "free stuff" and download the manual — my gift to you.

VISUALIZATIONS

As mentioned in Section Four, it is as important to clear the clutter in your mind as it is to clear the clutter in your environment. Below is an easy, step-by-step guide with some visualizations for you to tape and use. Remember, it only takes 20 minutes, three times a week, to work.

Following is a visualization process I have found very beneficial for clearing inner clutter. Each visualization involves three steps. Steps one and two are the same for all visualizations. Step three changes depending on your focus — achieving your goals, overcoming stress, or deep cleansing.

1. Relax using a breathing technique.

2. Cleanse the mind and body using the process of visualization. I use the Golden Light meditation described below. (There are many versions of the Golden Light meditation, but this is one I developed inspired by another Feng Shui teacher.)

3. Select and perform the visualization needed at that time. I have included three visualizations for you to try — achieving goals, connecting with power, and deep cleansing. ("Achieving Goals" is a variation of a meditation that I learned in the book *Secrets of Creative Visualization;* "Accessing Power" is my own and "Deep Cleansing" is inspired by another Feng Shui teacher.)

I suggest that you tape the process so that you can just listen to my words and go with the instructions. You may wish to tape this three times, repeating steps one and two and selecting one step three each time.

To ready yourself, choose a room where you will not be disturbed.

Close the door. Perhaps lower the lights. Lie down or sit in a comfortable position.

Here are the visualizations. Start your taping here.

1. Relax:

Concentrate on your breathing. Clear your mind of any thoughts. Breathe in, breathe out. Think only about your breathing and start to feel your body and mind relaxing. Breathe in power; breathe out negative energy and problems. To breathe in power, imagine sunlight entering your body. To breathe out negative energy, imagine dark shapes leaving your body. Allow yourself to relax; give yourself permission to relax.

2. Cleanse:

Now it is time to start a process of cleansing. Take your time with this process. Imagine a disc of golden light rotating above your head. Imagine a cone of golden light coming out of the disc and shining over you. Slowly see/feel or hear the disc rotating and entering your head — filling your mind with bright golden light that is pure, powerful and healing; filling all your thoughts and your inner mind with a bright golden light. As this light continues down through your body, allow it to linger in any areas that seem blocked and are dark. Imagine the disc slowly rotating down through your eyes, nose, ears and mouth, filling everything with bright light. Now the disc rotates slowly down your neck and into your chest. Your lungs are filled with light, healing and bright. Your heart is surrounded and filled with light that is healing and powerful. The disc rotates slowly into your abdomen, filling all your organs with bright, healing, golden light. Slowly it moves past your hips, down your thighs, past your knees, down your calves, past your ankles and feet and into the ground. The light moves back up slowly — filling everything once again with the bright, golden, healing light that is powerful and cleansing — until it is once again above your head. Imagine the cone of light shining over your body, covering the entire outside of your body. You are now filled and covered by the golden, bright, healing and powerful light.

3. Three Visualizations

#1: Achieving your goals.

Imagine that there is a heavy door in front of you and on the door is your name. As you reach out and touch it, the door will open. Walk through the door. You find yourself in a large room lit with all the colours of the rainbow. In the centre of the room is a pool, which is deep and glistening. Walk slowly towards it until you are standing right in front of it. The pool glows with power and shines with light. Light the candle, which is floating on the pool and is a symbolic representation of your inner power — your inner mind.

Focus your mind on the central pool and concentrate on your goals. See your goals written on a piece of paper and read them to yourself. Imagine the piece of paper floating down into the pool. The colours of the rainbow begin to agitate the pool and it forms a fountain. This fountain of water pours out of the heavy door, taking your goals with it. Follow your goals out of the room and close the heavy door. Know that the Universe will help you achieve your goals. Feel secure in this knowledge — all the creative power of the Universe is working with you to achieve your goals.

Express gratitude to the Universe for helping you achieve these goals.

It is time to slowly return to ordinary reality. Slowly bring your attention to your breath. In . . . out . . . in . . . out . . . . Wiggle your fingers and toes. Rub your hands together and rub the back of your neck to make yourself grounded again.

#2: Accessing power to overcome stresses in your life

Imagine that you are floating in the centre of a huge bubble. Below you is the earth, blue and green. You can see awesome mountaintops, glistening lakes and lush forests. Above you are the sun and the stars — think about their enormous power. Allow these huge forces to work in your life. Form a wonderful picture of the earth below and the sky above. Relax and receive the power of the Universe. This power is yours and will help you overcome stresses and struggles in your life. Allow yourself to fully receive this power. . . .

Express gratitude to the Universe for giving you your power.

It is time to slowly return to ordinary reality. Slowly bring your attention to your breath. In . . . out . . . in . . . out . . . . Wiggle your fingers and toes. Rub your hands together and rub the back of your neck to make yourself grounded again.

#3: Deep cleansing

Breathe deeply, concentrate on your breathing. Go to your safe place. This is a real or imagined place that is outdoors, where the sun is always shining, the sky is always blue, it is always peaceful and safe. Notice that there is a path leading out of the safe place and follow the trail. Walk along this beautiful path — there are birds and bunnies, beautiful flowers and tall healthy trees. Turn a corner and walk straight through a golden screen, which is in the middle of the walkway. As you pass through, feel your negative energy left behind you in the form of dust on the screen and collect this dust in your hand. Continue along the beautiful path until you reach a still, deep pool. Step onto a rock, which is hanging over the pool, drop the dust into the water and as it hits the water, watch it transform into millions of sparkles, which re-enter your body. Continue walking along the side of the pool, noticing the ducks, insects, fish and water lilies. You will come to a waterfall. Stand under the waterfall and allow it to flow over and through you, cleansing all your cells of negative energy until there is no more dark stuff coming out of the ends of your toes. Watch the water coming out of your toes change from dark to clear. Notice that there is a cave behind the waterfall, sparkling and beautiful. Enter the cave and receive a gift, which has been left there for you. Express gratitude to the Universe for cleansing your energy. Follow the path back to your safe place — through the waterfall, past the pool, past the golden screen. This path brings you back to this time and space.

It is time to slowly return to ordinary reality. Slowly bring your attention to your breath. In . . . out . . . in . . . out . . . . Wiggle your fingers and toes. Rub your hands together and rub the back of your neck to make yourself grounded again.

COLOUR IN YOUR HOME

Colour is a wonderful cure for energy problems in your home. It is also one of the quickest ways to enhance the Chi. Use the corresponding colour of the Bagua map for that area in your home by painting the walls or placing items of that colour in the zones. You will be amazed at how quickly you can change the energy and atmosphere in your home with a little paint. Remember that any shade of the particular colour will work. For example, the colour for the Family zone is green.

You could try hunter green or even the other end of the spectrum, a pastel green such as mint green.

Zone Colours

- Prosperity – red, purple and green

- Fame – red

- Relationships and Love – pink, red and white

- Creativity and Children – white

- Helpful People and Travel – grey, black and white

- Career and Life Path – dark blue and black

- Skills and Knowledge – blue, green and black

- Family – green and blue

- Health – yellow and earth tones.

There are certain meanings that the Chinese give to certain colours:

- Red means happiness, energy and good chi

- Pink means love and romance

- Purple means nobility, richness and power

- Blue could be positive or negative and means hope or mourning

- Green is for new growth and peace

- Yellow means wisdom, patience and tolerance

- Orange signifies happiness and power; peach, attraction and romance

- Brown means sturdiness and stability

- Tan is for new beginnings

- Black could be positive or negative and means spiritual and intellectual depth or depression

- Grey could mean harmony or frustration.

(Refer to Sarah Rossbach's book, *Interior Design with Feng Shui*, Chapter 9, for a more detailed listing.)

If it isn't appropriate to paint your home according to the colours of the Bagua map, other colours that work well for specific rooms are: light colours, pastels or white for the foyer; pink, blue or green for the master bedroom; white with red and black accents for the kitchen; green and blue for the children's bedrooms; earth tones, green or blue for the living room and family room; pink, blue or green for the dining room (although black and white will encourage weight loss); pastels or black and white for the bathrooms.

There are many choices for introducing effective colour into your home. If you choose not to paint the walls following the Bagua map guide, be sure to introduce the zone colours into that area in other ways, for instance using cushions, rugs, accents, flowers, etc. Many of our homes are aseptic and boring. Why not have fun with colour instead! Rich velvet colours will improve your Chi and the Chi of everyone who lives with you.

FIVE ELEMENT CHART

WOOD

Element	**Wood Chi**
Zone	Family and Prosperity
Colour	Green
Shape	Rectangular (upright tree trunk)

Characteristics   Expansive, growing, flexible, tough, creating, upward movement, energetic, determined

Cures   Healthy thriving plants or silk plants. Wooden furniture. Wood paneling. Natural fibers e.g. cotton, silk. Floral prints on: upholstery, wallpaper, curtains. Artwork: landscapes, gardens, flowers. Green or 'tree trunk' shaped items

Building Element Water   **Reducing Element** Metal

FIRE

Element	**Fire Chi**
Zone	Fame
Colour	Red
Shape	Triangle

Characteristics   Hot, explosive, bright, clear, enlightened

Cures   Candles. Fireplaces. Bright lights and lamps. Things made from animals (fur, leather, wool). Pets. Artwork: animals, people, sunlight or fire (e.g., volcanoes). Red or triangular shaped items

Building Element Wood   **Reducing Element** Water

EARTH

Element	**Earth Chi**
Zone	Health, Relationships & Love, and Skills & Knowledge
Colour	Yellow
Shape	Horizontal, square, flat

Characteristics   Stable, reliable, firm, centered, receptive, nourishing, romantic, still, growing, careful

Cures   Ceramic or earthenware. Brick or tile. Artwork: landscapes. Earth tone items or flat, square shaped items

Building Element Fire   **Reducing Element** Wood

METAL

Element	**Metal Chi**
Zone	Creativity & Children, and Helpful People & Travel
Colour	White
Shape	Circular, oval

Characteristics   Contracting, creative, heavy, energetic

Cures   All types of metals including stainless steel, copper, brass, iron, silver and gold. Natural crystals, rocks, gemstones, stones (marble, granite, flagstone). White items or oval and circular shaped items

Building Element Earth   **Reducing Element** Fire

WATER

Element	**Water Chi**
Zone	Career and Life Path
Colour	Black, dark blue
Shape	Undulating, free-form, a shape that fills the space just like water does

Characteristics   Deep, thoughtful, fluid, reflective, still

Cures   Streams, pools, fountains and water features. Crystal, glass and mirrors. Items that are black (charcoal or dark blue too) and have a flowing, free-form shape

Building Element Metal   **Reducing Element** Earth

BAGUA MAP

There are many instances throughout the book where I have suggested that you place a coloured Bagua map in a certain position in your environment. The Bagua map on the cover of this book has been modified by myself from many Bagua maps. Feel free to colour-copy and laminate my Bagua map. I give it to you with my blessing for a very powerful cure. Refer to page 23 and 45 for the black and white Bagua map.

ANNOTATED BIBLIOGRAPHY

1. *Clear Your Clutter with Feng Shui,* Karen Kingston, Broadway Books, New York, NY and Judy Piatkus (Publishers) Ltd., London, UK, 1998.

   Karen Kingston is a favourite author of mine on BTB Feng Shui. She specializes in removing clutter and this book will give you every tool you need to get your clutter under control.

2. *The Everything Numerology Book,* Ellae Elinwood, Adams Media Corporation, Avon, MA, 2003.

   It is not only the simple way in which it is written, but also the easy-to-read layout that makes this the only numerology book that I have recommended. A great resource for the novice and expert.

3. *Feng Shui for Dummies*, David Daniel Kennedy, Hungry Minds, Inc., New York, NY, 2001.

   David Daniel Kennedy is a renowned BTB Feng Shui specialist. This is a great reference book for your Feng Shui library.

4. *Feng Shui Your Kitchen*, Sharon Stasney, A Sterling/Chapelle Book, Sterling Publishing Co. Inc., New York, NY, 2002.

   In this book (pp. 36, 37) Sharon Stasney includes a simple and fun exercise for finding out what your personal element is. A great exercise to do with your partner and friends. Note though — this is not a BTB Feng Shui book.

5. *The Four Agreements*, Don Miguel Ruiz, A Toltec Wisdom Book, Amber Allen Publishing, San Rafael, CA, 1997.

   To be touched by Don Miguel Ruiz is an honour in itself. The Four Agreements is compulsory reading for anyone trying to get their life into the Feng Shui Zone.

6. *Harmonise Your Home*, Graham Gunn, An Orion Paperback, Orion Books Ltd., London, UK, 1999.

   Graham Gunn provided me with a terrific look at the other schools of Feng Shui and some solid advice on becoming a published Feng Shui author.

7. *Inner and Outer Peace through Meditation*, Rajinder Singh, Element, Harper Collins Publishers, London, UK.

   Chapter 4 provides an excellent step-by-step guide to meditation, written by one of the world's leading teachers of meditation and contributors to world peace.

8. *Interior Design with Feng Shui*, Sarah Rossbach, Compass, Penguin Group, New York, NY, 1987.

   One of the earliest Feng Shui writers, Sarah Rossbach provides a comprehensive look at Feng Shui and colour in Chapter 9.

9. *The Modern Book of Feng Shui*, Steven Post, A Byron Preiss Book, Dell Publishing, New York, NY, 1998.

A student of Professor Lin Yun, the author provides a valuable resource. This is a more advanced look at BTB Feng Shui.

10. *Move Your Stuff, Change your Life,* Karen Rauch Carter, A Fireside Book, Simon & Schuster, Inc., New York, NY, 2000.

    By far, this is my favourite BTB Feng Shui book, and it is the book I recommend most often to people just starting to be interested in Feng Shui.

11. *The Secrets of Creative Visualization,* Philip Cooper, Samuel Weiser, Inc., York Beach, ME, 1999.

    This is just a wonderful, simple and easy-to-follow resource for visualization.

12. *Supernature,* Lyall Watson, Coronet Books, Hodder and Stoughton Limited, London, UK, 1973.

    Written so long ago, this book is still so full of incredible stories and wisdom. Reading it will expand your mind.

13. *Teach Yourself I Ching,* Andy Baggott, A Teach Yourself Book, NTC/Contemporary Publishing, Chicago, IL, 1999.

    In my opinion, this is the ultimate book on I Ching. The key to the success of this interpretation lies in the descriptions of the meanings.

14. *The Curve of Time,* M. Wylie Blanchet, Gray's Publishing, Sidney, British Columbia, 1968.

    No annotation

INTERNET RESOURCES

Emotional Freedom Technique: www.emofree.com

BTB Feng Shui: www.yunlintemple.org

My website for *In the Feng Shui Zone*: www.fengshui-zone.com

FENG SHUI ITEMS AVAILABLE

Besides being available in bookstores, this book and the Feng Shui items mentioned throughout are available for sale through my website www.fengshui-zone.com or by emailing me at fengshuizone@shaw.ca

These items include:

In the Feng Shui Zone   Bagua mirrors

Crystals   Laminated Baguas

MAKING CONTACT

I enjoy assisting others in becoming passionate about Feng Shui. I do this by:

1. Individual sessions: either in person or by telephone.

2. For those who enjoy learning in person, I offer workshops for beginners as well as more experienced Feng Shui-ers.

3. I offer a course for students wanting to become Feng Shui Practitioners (those who wish to do Feng Shui for others). This Practitioner Course includes an apprenticeship and is done by telephone and correspondence.

4. I am an approved educator for Real Estate Agents who need help with solving Feng Shui problems for their clients.

If you are interested in attending a workshop or hosting me to give a workshop for any size group, I can be reached at:

E-mail: fengshuizone@shaw.ca   Website: www. fengshui-zone.com

The publisher of this book can be reached at:

Granville Island Publishing,

212 – 1656 Duranleau, Vancouver, BC, Canada V6H 3S4

(604) 688-0320, 1-877-688-0320

Website: www.granvilleislandpublishing.com

ABOUT THE AUTHOR

Debra Ford is an international Feng Shui Practitioner and de-Cluttering coach offering home, office and retail Feng Shui services. Debra teaches Feng Shui at a community college, writes for women's publications, teaches real estate professionals how to work with clients who have Feng Shui needs (including preparing homes for a quick sale), hosts workshops and provides consultation services for home make-overs and office de-cluttering. Debra may be contacted at fengshuizone@shaw.ca. Debra is a third generation African and was born in Durban, South Africa. She has been happily married for over 20 years and is the mother and 'Chi' guardian of two sons. Debra and her family now live in Calgary, Alberta, Canada.

In the Feng Shui Zone will change your life; it's about using a "tried and tested" ancient Chinese art and science to effect improvements in your life that you never dreamed possible. *In the Feng Shui Zone* is practical, simple and easy to follow and includes a Nine Step guide to getting your home and your life into the zone.